The Civil Defense Book

The Civil Defense Book

Emergency Preparedness for a Rural or Suburban Community

Michael Mabee

Contact the author at: CivilDefenseBook@gmail.com
www.CivilDefenseBook.com

ISBN-13: 9781974320943
ISBN-10: 1974320944

Library of Congress Control Number: 2017914303
CreateSpace Independent Publishing Platform
North Charleston, South Carolina

Note: The first edition of this book was published on July 4, 2013 as *Prepping for a Suburban or Rural Community: Building a Civil Defense Plan for a Long-Term Catastrophe.* (ISBN: 1482731215 / ISBN-13: 9781482731217 Library of Congress Control Number: 2013904810.)

Disclaimer: This book is not intended to give legal advice and is intended to provide general information only. While every effort was made to insure the accuracy of the information contained herein, the author and publisher shall have neither liability nor responsibility for any alleged harm arising directly or indirectly from the use of information in this book.

Dedication

To my precious wife Sandy,

It never dawned on me when I saved your life in 1987, that you would in return rescue me in 2014.

It's always been you.

Acknowledgements

This book was inspired in part by a proposed House Resolution. (I wonder how often that happens.) I would like to thank the bipartisan sponsors of House Resolution 762 (112th Congress): Roscoe G. Bartlett (R-MD), Yvette D. Clarke (D-NY), Trent Franks (R-AZ) and Hank Johnson (D-GA).

While the resolution may have died in committee, I hope the idea doesn't.

I would also like to acknowledge the Commission to Assess the Threat to the United States from Electromagnetic Pulse (EMP) Attack. I fear that too few Americans have heard of the EMP Commission and their critically important work. But every American—and every politician—should pay close attention to the findings and recommendations of the EMP Commission and the very real threats to the power grid.

Thanks to Ellen Jarus Hanley for your editorial expertise and friendship.

Finally, thanks to my copy editor (Mom). I doubt she envisioned that her spawn would be so bad at singular possessives. Thanks Mom. At least now I have someone else to blame for any errant apostrophes that slipped through.

A Note on the Kindle Edition

If the grid goes down, so does your Kindle, Nook, iPad or other e-reader. Any useful books on preparedness and survival you find, you will want to have in hard copy for reference when you really need them. In fact, any that you find extremely useful, you may want to consider having more than one copy. Knowledge may be more valuable than currency someday.

I think that all prepping and survival books should have very inexpensive e-book editions. If people find them useful, they are going to buy a hard copy. If not, they won't.

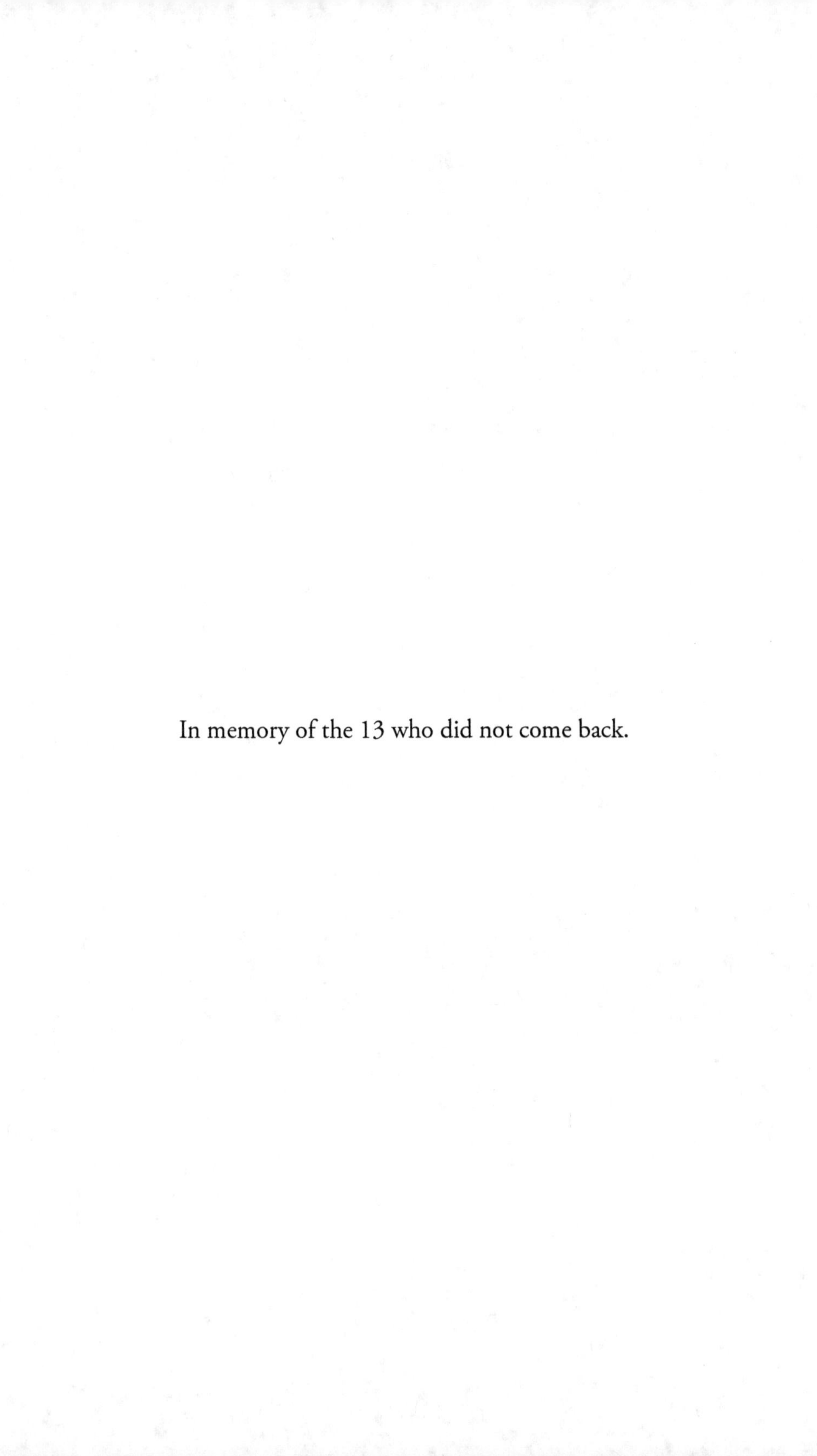

In memory of the 13 who did not come back.

Contents

Preface

This quote is from a 2017 report from the Senate Committee on Homeland Security and Governmental Affairs[1]:

"C. CRITICAL INFRASTRUCTURE
The United States depends on its critical infrastructure, particularly the electric power grid, as all critical infrastructure sectors are to some degree dependent on electricity to operate. A successful nuclear electromagnetic pulse (EMP) attack against the United States <u>could cause the death of approximately 90 percent of the American population</u>. Similarly, a geomagnetic disturbance (GMD) could have equally devastating effects on the power grid." [emphasis added]

Huh? Are you kidding me? Did anybody notice this and is Congress doing anything about this? The answers, unfortunately, are: few people noticed it and no, Congress isn't doing anything about it. So, here's the deal:

Preppers: Your "bug out bag" and a year's worth of pinto beans in Mylar® pouches are not going to save you.

Everybody else: If you don't believe or have never considered that our electrical grid is extremely vulnerable—and that the loss of the electrical grid for a prolonged period of time could result in tens of millions of deaths and could

---

1 U.S. Senate. *Activities of the Committee on Homeland Security and Governmental Affairs. Report 115-12.* 115th Congress (March 28, 2017).

catapult the United States technologically back over a century—you may want to review the congressional hearings and the reports of the EMP Commission listed in the references section (links are provided to these documents). I'm not here to convince you. Decide for yourself.

What kind of long-term catastrophe is possible? In one scenario discussed at numerous U.S. congressional hearings, an electromagnetic pulse (EMP), delivered either from a solar flare or a terrorist EMP weapon, could cause up to 90 percent of the U.S. population to die, and everybody left would be thrown back to a nineteenth-century (i.e., the 1800s) agricultural society— our iPads never to return. And that is just one of several possible scenarios that could create a national catastrophe.

Let's back up. When we hear the term "nuclear war" what comes to mind for most people is the Cold War era specter of cities laid to waste by ICBMs and nothing surviving except the cockroaches. But while the threat of that type of war is less worrisome today to most people than it was in the 1960s and 1970s, there is another worry. Today, one terrorist missile with a small nuclear warhead fired from a ship could take down the power grid. And it is possible that the grid would never come back. That is the threat of an EMP weapon. And it doesn't have to be terrorists. The sun can do much the same thing to the grid with a solar flare of the magnitude that happens every 100 years or so. How long has it been since the last one? Over 100 years.

I've worked as an urban EMT and paramedic. I've worked as a suburban cop and for the federal government. I've had a good deal of military train-ing, two wartime deployments to Iraq, and two humanitarian deployments to Guatemala. Hell, I was even in the Boy Scouts as a kid. So, if you asked me a few years ago if I was "prepared," I would say that I was more prepared than most.

If you ask me now if I am prepared, I'd have to say no.

Although I am personally as prepared as I can be, that is not good enough. Individual preparedness and family preparedness alone are not going to save us in a long-term national catastrophe. That is the purpose of this book. Instead of focusing, as many "lone wolf" preppers do, solely on individual and fam-ily preparedness, wouldn't we be better off to also focus on the survival of our town or village? Wouldn't prepping be better played as a team sport?

A year's worth of food storage will do you little good if your house is looted by a heavily armed group of desperate, starving refugees in a "without rule of law" world. But if you live in a fairly secure town, with a working preparedness plan (which includes an adequate security force), there is a better chance that your family's preparedness supplies—and your family—would survive. Moreover, it does not matter how much food and water you have saved up; eventually, you are going to run out, even if you are not looted. Then what? If your town has an effective government and a contingency plan for security, food, water, and medical care ("beans, bullets, and bandages"), everybody's survival prospects in the town increase.

Most families will be unable, realistically, to have a doctor, dentist, farmer, soldier, carpenter, teacher, alternative energy expert, horticulturalist, brick mason, and blacksmith in their houses. But the community at large has all these resources.

So "community prepping"—in addition to individual and family prepping—has the advantages of collective resources, collective skills, and collective security. Individual and family preparedness alone isn't going to cut it if the grid goes down for a year or more. A prepared family in a prepared community has a much greater chance of survival. There is another term for "community prepping": civil defense.

Let's say the power goes out for a year or more (and there are several realistic scenarios in which this could occur). Would you rather be on your own, with no government, and everybody else as a potential enemy out to get your #10 cans of pinto beans? Or would you rather go to sleep secure (and perhaps even warm) knowing that there is a sufficient security force on duty, crops in the fields, and medical personnel available if needed; knowing that people's basic needs for food, water, shelter, and medical care were, at least on a basic level, being addressed; knowing that you have a role in your community's survival, whether it be as a nurse, security force member, carpenter, or [name your role here]?

In a national catastrophe, many people—including individual preppers—would end up as refugees for one reason or another. There are few people who have a cabin hundreds of miles away, deep in the woods, where they can "bug out" and no human will ever find them; where they can get clean water from a stream, and game is always plentiful; where they can wait out the "apocalypse" in safety and live off the land. It's just not realistic for the majority of us.

It is equally unrealistic that we can survive for long, no matter how prepared we purport to be, alone in our houses in the suburbs or rural areas of America. We need each other. We need collective skills and resources. We need other people who have our backs.

So if the power goes out for a year or more, where would you rather be? Town X, which has been looted and overrun by starving, desperate refugees, has lost all of its precious resources, and has nobody (or an opportunistic criminal) in charge or Town Y, which planned ahead, activated a catastrophe plan on day one, and has security, resources, an effective democratic government, and people looking out for each other?

To me, it's a no-brainer. This book is about being Town Y.

Many preppers have read William R. Forstchen's novel *One Second After*, but one of the central lessons, in my opinion, has been lost on many. This lesson is that the *community* and people working together are the key to survival. If you want yourself and your family to be among the 10 percent who survive, you need to pay attention: The town of Black Mountain had the advantages of time and geography (not to mention a protagonist with some knowledge and leadership skills). The town was able to organize and pull together after the fact. Most communities will not be that lucky and so they need to prepare ahead of time if they wish to survive. Time and geography are not on the side of many, especially in suburban communities.

There are many books out there on preparedness. However, most of these focus on individual and family preparedness; there is little out there on what a community can do in a long-term catastrophe and how to prepare ahead of time. Specifically, I have not been able to find a template or "plan" that can be tailored to fit and adopted. FEMA advocates community preparedness but has not provided a comprehensive how-to on what towns should do in a worst-case scenario.[2] What if the federal and state governments just can't help your

---

2 FEMA's Emergency Support Function (ESF) #14 "Long-Term Community Recovery" assumes the availability of outside resources and agencies. This is not a criticism of the ESF, but it simply

town for months or years, due to a catastrophe of national-scale? This book will attempt to provide a road map to fill that gap.

You still should read all the individual preparedness books you can get your hands on. The more you know, and the more skills you have, the more useful you can be to your community.

A quick note on communities: A friend of mine who lives over on the "left coast" pointed out that some of what is written here might not fly with people in his area. He's absolutely correct. What works in rural "Red State" might not work in suburban "Blue State." There is nothing wrong with that. This book is not about the right way to prep—it is intended to show one way to prep. There is only one wrong way to prep: that is, not to prepare at all.

We Americans are generations removed from adversity and generations removed from self-reliance. This makes us weak. Anybody who lived through the great depression is in their 80s or 90s now. The rest of us were born and grew up dependent on technology, specifically the power grid. We are not self-reliant—we are grid-reliant. Everything is fine as long as all our infrastructures work—food, water, sanitation, medical care and our government. But all of these infrastructures, including basic rule of law, are completely dependent on the power grid. The majority of people don't think of it: without the electric grid, there is no food, no water, no sewers, no sanitation and quickly degrading medical care and rule of law. We are not just weak, we are addicts. The majority of us will literally die of starvation and disease if we lose the grid long-term.

So, let me end the preface and begin the book with a question: What could possibly be worse than a nuclear war where we all die instantly? One where we don't.

That's what we should prepare for.

---

would be overwhelmed if most or all communities in the U.S. were in trouble at the same time. See: http://www.fema.gov/pdf/emergency/nrf/nrf-esf-14.pdf (accessed September 1, 2017).

One

The Need for Community Prepping (Civil Defense)

Personal Lessons Learned from Minor Power Outages

Everybody has experienced a power outage at one time or another. Usually, they are merely an inconvenience. On August 14, 2003, I was at my desk in New York City when the Great Northeast Blackout hit and 50 million people in the U.S. and Canada lost power. At the time, I was living on Long Island. Getting home from the city to my suburban home was an ordeal. This power outage—which, while massive, only lasted a few days—really got me thinking. Years before, I had bought a generator "just in case." After this outage, I had an electrician install a connection to my house so I could run the entire house from the generator.[3] That was about six moves ago. Ever since then, at every house I have lived in, I have had a generator connection hardwired to the house. I also have gotten in the habit of keeping a full get-home bag at my office and in my vehicle. I also have "EDC" (every day carry) items that I have with me at all times—in my pockets and my bookbag.[4]

Fast forward a few years. I moved from New York to a planned unit development of about eighty houses on the border between "suburban" and "rural" Connecticut. On October 29, 2011, a massive ice storm hit the Northeast and over two million households lost power. My neighborhood (and most of the surrounding towns) lost power for over a week.

---

3 See my video "Running a House from a Generator" on YouTube: https://youtu.be/hdufshn6S9U

4 See my video on "EDC" on YouTube: https://youtu.be/cM6TsGC5iPg

By the time the power came back on, over half of the houses in the development were abandoned, as they were uninhabitable. The development had a low-pressure sewer system. This means each house had a 240-volt grinder pump in the basement, immersed in an enclosed sewage tank. When one took a shower or flushed the toilet, the water went into the tank and, when it got to a certain level, the pump kicked on, "pureed" the contents of the tank, and pumped the sewage out through a small 1¼-inch pipe into the town sewer system.

From what I understood, there had not been a significant power outage in the neighborhood since they began constructing these houses in 2001; I moved there in 2010. So, when the power went out in 2011, many people, not realizing the consequences, continued to use their water and flush their toilets. Soon the tanks overflowed and raw sewage flowed into their basements. Some people realized what would happen and stopped using their water. The effect was the same: over eighty houses with no electricity, no heat, no water, and no sewer. Uninhabitable. Even for the few who were lucky enough to find a generator during the outage, there is no way to hook up a generator to these grinder pumps without having an electrician hardwire it into the house.

And good luck trying to find an electrician with all the necessary parts during a major power outage.

Mine was one of the only houses (if not *the* only house) in the development that had a generator hardwired into the electrical system before the storm. Because all of my appliances (heat, hot water, stove, and dryer) were natural gas, I could easily run the entire house—including the grinder pump—on a 5500-watt gasoline generator.

Gasoline for the generator immediately became a potential issue: the generator's tank holds seven gallons, and I had two full five-gallon gas cans (I use STA-BIL° fuel stabilizer and rotate the gas by dumping into my truck every September). Also, I had figured on the fact that my car held 12 gallons, and my truck held 24. When the storm hit, all the gas stations in my town and the surrounding towns were out of power. I soon realized that I could not siphon gas from the vehicles, as I had planned. (Apparently, there is something on newer vehicles that prevents you from doing this.) To run my generator for 24 hours takes 8 to 10 gallons of gas. So, essentially, I only had a day-and-a-half supply (17 gallons), when I thought I would have an additional three-to four-day supply (36 gallons) available in the cars, if needed. I did a reconnaissance and found no gas stations that had power in my town or the next towns over.

I listened to the radio and learned of a few open gas stations in our area of the state. With the generator on its last tank, I set off with my two empty 5-gallon jerry cans to find gas several towns away. (By the way, don't ever bet that you are going to find additional 5-gallon gas cans in stock at the hardware store or Home Depot in the middle of a major power outage.)

The scene at the open gas station got me thinking about how thin the veneer of civilization is. People were stressed, ornery, and, in some cases, violent. There were fights. People were acting crazy. This was only a bad power outage, for Pete's sake, not the apocalypse. The power would be coming back on eventually!

I waited in line, got my gas, and left. After the first trip, I made a habit of going back at five in the morning every day to avoid the crowds. I also began thinking about what would happen if the power went off for a long time. What would people be like? What would *life* be like?

I always had a good amount of food in the house, and a stocked freezer in the garage, so I was fine for the week. I had food, water, and power. I could even do laundry and use the central vac. Next door, the neighbors had to abandon their house and move in with relatives until power was restored. Some minor preparedness enabled me to dodge the small bullet of a short-term power outage.

Prior to the power outage, I think I was what you might call a "FEMA 72-hour guy"—more prepared than the majority of the people. After the power came back, I purchased additional 5-gallon gas cans and a 29-gallon Tempo Gas Walker for the future. I started to think about what I would do if there was a longer power outage. What would happen if the whole grid went down for a long period?

A few observations:

- Modern houses are problematic without power. None of the houses in my neighborhoods during the 2003 and 2011 outages had wood stoves or fireplaces. (A few have natural gas fireplaces, but if the gas goes you're out of luck.) There is no heat for most people without electricity (and even gas and oil furnaces require electricity).

- Water and sewage systems do not work without power. Although you may retain "city water" and "city sewer" service in a minor outage, if the grid goes down long-term, the water and sewer will go off. If you have a well, you probably have an electric pump. Some septic systems also have an electric pump, but at a minimum you need water to flush the toilet.

- Adequate food storage is critical, but eventually you are going to run out. With no grid, the supply chain will be disrupted. How much of what you buy at the grocery store comes from the town you live in?

- Fuel may not be available. Refineries need power. Once the gas stations' tanks are empty—if you can figure out a way to pump out the gas—no more trucks are coming for a long time.

- Natural gas, propane, and home heating oil may not be available. (Same as above—no supply chain, no fuel).

- What are you going to do without transportation? (Even if an EMP does not fry your car's computer chips, there will soon be no gas.)

- Look to Hurricane Katrina for what can happen to the medical system in a regional catastrophe.[5] Now imagine what happens if it is a national catastrophe, and nobody is coming to help. If the hospitals don't have power, and the supply chain for medications and supplies is disrupted, the systems will fail. Moreover, with transportation

---

5 See, for example: Lister, Sarah A. *The Public Health and Medical Response to Disasters: Federal Authority and Funding*, Washington: Congressional Research Service, August 1, 2008. https://fas. org/sgp/crs/misc/RL33579.pdf (accessed: September 1, 2017).

affected, patients will have limited means of obtaining even rudimentary care.

- Don't count on desperate people being congenial. Security is critical; looting and crime are huge issues, even in regional disasters. Rule of law is fragile. (There are only 7 cops in my town, including the Chief of Police!)
- A national catastrophe will be "come as you are." Whatever you (and your town) don't have now will be difficult or impossible to get later.

Bottom line: if the grid goes down for a long period of time, we're screwed. But we don't have to be.

What Would Happen if the Whole Grid Went Down?

In 2004, the Commission to Assess the Threat to the United States from Electromagnetic Pulse (EMP) Attack issued a report that summarized the effect of an EMP attack on the United States:

Depending on the specific characteristics of the attacks, unprecedented cascading failures of our major infrastructures could result. In that event, a regional or national recovery would be long and difficult and would seriously degrade the safety and overall viability of our Nation. The primary avenues for catastrophic damage to the Nation are through our electric power infrastructure and thence into our telecommunications, energy, and other infrastructures. These, in turn, can seriously impact other important aspects of our Nation's life, including the financial system; means of getting food, water, and medical care to the citizenry; trade; and production of goods and services. The recovery of any one of the key national infrastructures is dependent on the recovery of others. The longer the outage, the more problematic and uncertain the recovery will be. It is possible for the functional outages to become mutually reinforcing until at some point the degradation of infrastructure could have irreversible effects on the country's ability to support its population.[6]

The nation's ability to support the population depends on several interdependent systems—all of which depend on the power grid. Put simply, if the power grid were to go down for a substantial period of time, there would be no way to get food, water, fuel, sanitation, medicine, and other essential services to the population. These conditions would have "irreversible effects on the country's ability to support any large fraction of its present human population."[7]

Past power outages, even fairly big ones, have been temporary, but lack of food, water, and basic services even in regional outages have caused riots and a breakdown in law and order. And these were only temporary blackouts. Dr. Peter Vincent Pry, senior staff of the Congressional EMP Commission, compared recent incidents experienced in the United States to a potential long-term catastrophe:

It didn't become a catastrophe because of the edge effect, because we were able to move in there, and also because it was just the power grid that was down, in the case of New York, and so fairly easily repairable. It could be repaired in a week or two.

But if you extrapolate something like that happening for months or years, you are obviously talking about a life-threatening kind of a catastrophe because you cannot endure, or you cannot support the population without food, without water for those protracted periods of time, nor can one count on societal stability for protracted periods of time. I think the [Hurricane] Andrew experience in those eight counties, what happened there in terms of social cohesion is

---

6 Graham, William R. (Chairman), et al. *Report of the Commission to Assess the Threat to the United States from Electromagnetic Pulse (EMP) Attack*, Volume 1, Executive Report, (2004), pp. 1–2.

7 *Terrorism and the EMP Threat to Homeland Security, Before the US Senate, Subcommittee on Terrorism, Technology and Homeland Security of the Committee on the Judiciary*, 109th Congress, p. 13 (March 8, 2005) (statement of Dr. Lowell Wood, Commissioner, Congressional EMP Commission).

instructive in terms of what could happen on a national basis if such a disaster were to occur.[8]

In fact, in the EMP Commission report in 2008, the Commission noted:

Electrical power is necessary to support other critical infrastructures, including supply and distribution of water, food, fuel, communications, transport, financial transactions, emergency services, government services, and all other infrastructures supporting the national economy and welfare. Should significant parts of the electrical power infrastructure be lost for any substantial period of time, the Commission believes that the consequences are likely to be catastrophic, and many people may ultimately die for lack of the basic elements necessary to sustain life in dense urban and suburban communities. In fact, the Commission is deeply concerned that such impacts are likely in the event of an EMP attack unless practical steps are taken to provide protection for critical elements of the electric system and for rapid restoration of electric power, particularly to essential services.[9]

Is a National-Scale Catastrophe Possible?

Unfortunately, yes. There have been numerous congressional hearings and government studies that cover, in detail, the various threats to the power grid. (Links to several of these hearings and reports can be found in the References Section.) Here is a brief summary of a few frequently discussed threats to the power grid:

---

8 *Terrorism and the EMP Threat to Homeland Security, Before the US Senate, Subcommittee on Terrorism, Technology and Homeland Security of the Committee on the Judiciary,* 109th Congress, p. 19 (March 8, 2005) (statement of Dr. Peter Pry, senior staff, Congressional EMP Commission).

9 Graham, William R. (Chairman), et al. *Report of the Commission to Assess the Threat to the United States from Electromagnetic Pulse (EMP) Attack: Critical National Infrastructures.* (April 2008), p. vii.

- We have been attacked in the past by terrorists. Few doubt that there are those who would like to attack us again. In fact, "al-Qa'ida and other terrorist groups are known to have considered energy facilities—and other infrastructure facilities—as possible targets."[10] A terrorist attack on the power grid could be devastating.

- There have been massive solar flares in the past, which, if they occurred today, could have a devastating, long-term effect on the power grid. In a report for FERC, DOE, and DHS, the Oak Ridge National Laboratory stated that if a storm of the magnitude observed in 1859 and 1921 occurred today, "it could interrupt power to as many as 130 million people in the United States alone, requiring several years to recover.[11] Note that in 1859 and 1921, we were not as dependent on electronics as we are today.

- Several countries already have or soon will have the capability of launching an electromagnetic pulse (EMP) weapon against the United States. An EMP weapon could severely damage or destroy the power grid. Terrorists could even launch such a weapon: "Earlier this year [2005], CIA Director Porter Goss gave chilling testimony about missing nuclear material from storage sites in Russia that may have found its way into terrorists' hands. FBI Director [Robert] Mueller confirmed new intelligence that suggests that al Qaeda is trying to acquire and use weapons of mass destruction in some form against us."[12] An EMP device launched from a freighter off the U.S. coast could take down the grid before our defenses could

---

10 *Implications of Power Blackouts for the Nation's Cybersecurity and Critical Infrastructure Protection, Before the US House, Joint Hearing of the Subcommittee on Cybersecurity, Science, and Research and Development, and the Subcommittee on Infrastructure and Border Security of the Select Committee on Homeland Security*, p. 11, 108th Congress (2003) (statement of Larry A. Mefford, executive assistant director, Counterterrorism and Counterintelligence, Federal Bureau of Investigation).

11 Oak Ridge National Laboratory, "Electromagnetic Pulse: Effects on the US Power Grid," Oak Ridge, TN (January, 2010), Executive Summary, p. 1.

12 *Terrorism and the EMP Threat to Homeland Security, Before the US Senate, Subcommittee on Terrorism, Technology, and Homeland Security of the Committee on the Judiciary* 109th Congress (March 8, 2005) (statement of Senator Jon Kyl).

react. In 2010, Senator Jon Kyl stated in a Congressional hearing: "Unfortunately, a successful EMP attack would not require a high level of military or nuclear sophistication. A relatively crude nuclear weapon mounted on a Scud missile, for example, could be launched from a ship in U.S. waters and inflict massive damage on the United States."[13]

- The Department of Energy lists pandemic as one of the "four main risk scenarios concerning the Electricity Subsector."[14] There have been pandemics in the past that have killed anywhere from tens of thousands to tens of millions of people. There will be more pandemics in the future. Because of air travel, pandemics may be more quickly and widely spread than in the past. We have not successfully cured every disease we have encountered. Failure of the power grid due to a pandemic involving a strain of disease that is highly contagious and resistant to treatment is not a far-fetched scenario.

- Large-scale natural disasters (including things like solar flares, earthquakes, a meteor strike, or massive volcanic eruptions) have happened in the past and are likely to happen in the future.[15]

- Economic collapses of entire countries have happened in the past. Just because we are the United States does not mean it can't happen here. We have come dangerously close on several occasions (and it is debatable if we've fixed the problems that caused those

---

13 *Government Preparedness and Response to a Terrorist Attack Using Weapons of Mass Destruction, Before the US Senate, Subcommittee on Terrorism, Technology and Homeland Security of the Committee on the Judiciary* hearing, 111th Congress (August 4, 2010) (S. Hrg. 111–884) (statement of Senator Jon Kyl).

14 US Department of Energy, Office of Electricity Delivery and Energy Reliability, *Large Power Transformers and the U.S. Electric Grid*, (June 2012), p. 3. http://energy.gov/sites/prod/files/Large%20Power%20Transformer%20Study%20-%20 June%202012_0.pdf (accessed August 28, 2017).

15 See, for example, *Protecting the Electric Grid: H.R. —————, The Grid Reliability and Infrastructure Defense Act, Before the US House, Subcommittee on Energy and Power of the Committee on Energy and Commerce*, 112th Congress (May 31, 2011) (statement of Joseph H. McClelland, Director of the Office of Electric Reliability, Federal Energy Regulatory Commission).

near financial meltdowns). Such an economic collapse could also threaten the power grid.

The purpose of this book isn't to predict which one will happen and when. The point is that all of the above things (except an actual attack by an EMP weapon) *have* happened in the past, and all could possibly happen in the future.

A localized disaster, such as the 9/11 terrorist attacks, which occurred in three local areas, can have a national impact, such as shutting down the nation's air travel for a period. On the other hand, Hurricane Katrina was a huge disaster, causing much death, destruction, and displacement of people in New Orleans and the Gulf Coast, but elsewhere in the country people did not feel the effect. In all past localized disasters in the U.S., resources were available from outside the affected areas because everywhere else the power was still on and there was still milk on the grocery store shelves.

So, it's easy for people to assume that, even if a disaster happens, somebody "out there" (e.g., the federal government, Red Cross, etc.) will come in to help the affected area, and the rest of us will be OK.

There are several scenarios in which we could have a national catastrophe that would overwhelm federal, state, and local governments and endanger a great portion of the U.S. population. None of these scenarios is far-fetched. You can decide for yourself how likely any particular scenario is, but, no matter the cause, the type of national catastrophe I am talking about here has two things in common:

1) Long-term disruption of the national power grid
2) Long-term disruption of the supply chain

For the purposes of this book, let's define a national catastrophe as an event in which the power grid is down for a year or more and the supply chain is interrupted for an equally long period of time.

Because the government does not have the ability to handle this worst-case-scenario national catastrophe, several members of Congress became concerned and attempted to bring attention to the problem by sponsoring a resolution on August 2, 2012. The resolution died in committee.[16]

Since that time, there has been more awareness of Electromagnetic Pulse (EMP) and Geomagnetic Disturbances (GMD) and numerous government reports and hearings have taken place. The government response has been flaccid over the last few decades—I describe it as "directyle dysfunction." Despite several Congressional attempts to protect the grid, the vast majority of which died in the legislature, only two minor pieces of legislation became law. Both were shoehorned in with defense appropriations bills:

- The National Defense Authorization Act for Fiscal Year 2016 re-established the Commission to Assess the Threat to the United States from Electromagnetic Pulse Attack.
- The National Defense Authorization Act for Fiscal Year 2017 will finally require the Department of Homeland Security to include EMP and GMD in Planning and Preparedness.

While these are both welcome developments, neither will protect the power grid tomorrow, or next year, or even several years from now. They are too little, too late and Congress needs to take more substantial action to protect the power grid.

Until then, we are all in grave danger.

What Can Happen Post-Catastrophe?

If the power grid were damaged by an EMP weapon or a solar flare, it could take years to recover. "Some critical electrical power infrastructure components

---

16 See Appendix 1 for the full text of H. Res. 762: "Expressing the sense of the House of Representatives regarding community-based civil defense and power generation."

are no longer manufactured in the United States, and their acquisition ordinarily requires up to a year of lead time in routine circumstances."[17]

Perhaps the most chilling description of life after an EMP (or solar flare, for that matter) comes from the testimony of Dr. Lowell Wood, Commissioner of the Congressional EMP Commission:

> When that type of weapon is exploded at several dozen to a few hundred kilometers above the United States, if it happened in the middle of the day, you might see or hear nothing. The lights would go out. A great deal of things instantly dependent on electricity would go away. And depending on the nature of the damage, its severity, its geographical descent, the lights might come back on hours later, they might come back on decades later. If they come back on in hours, as we know from blackouts, there is just a great deal of inconvenience and substantial economic loss. If the lights stay off for more than a year in this country, the Commission's estimate was the loss of life would run into the tens of millions, perhaps a great deal more. You miss the harvest. You have no refrigeration, no transportation, no anything except what we had as a country in the 1880's. Most Americans will die in that interval.[18]

Would local, state, or even federal government be able to maintain order? If localized disasters are any indication, the answer unfortunately is no. Even with massive state and federal assistance on the way, disasters like Katrina have demonstrated that civilization is fragile and rule of law is easily cast aside. In a scenario where, substantially, the entire country were without power for a long period of time, it is not a stretch to say that local and state governments would not be able to maintain order.

---

17 Graham, William R. (Chairman), et al. *Report of the Commission to Assess the Threat to the United States from Electromagnetic Pulse (EMP) Attack: Critical National Infrastructures.* (April 2008), p. vi.

18 *Terrorism and the EMP Threat to Homeland Security, Before the US Senate, Subcommittee on Terrorism, Technology and Homeland Security of the Committee on the Judiciary,* 109th Congress, p. 18 (March 8, 2005).

If you want to see an interesting depiction of what this might look like, the History Channel aired a docudrama in 2010 called *After Armageddon*, about life after a pandemic. (You can find it on the Internet or buy it from the History Channel's website.) In this film, the same issues that the United States would face in a loss of the electric grid are discussed by experts in the context of a global pandemic.[19]

In any catastrophe where the power and transportation infrastructures are affected for a long period of time, the consequences are dire:

> The heavy concentration of our population in urban and suburban areas has been enabled by the ability to continuously supply food from farms and processing centers far removed. Today, cities typically have a food supply of only several days available on grocery shelves for their customers. Replenishment of that food supply depends on a continuous flow of trucks from food processing centers to food distribution centers to warehouses and to grocery stores and restaurants. If urban food supply flow is substantially interrupted for an extended period of time, hunger and mass evacuation, even starvation and anarchy, could result.[20]

In the vacuum created by a lack of effective federal or state government assistance (exacerbated by lack of communications and supply chains during a long-term grid failure), the most effective government will be local. Problems will have to be solved locally.

Survival will be a local issue—the cavalry isn't coming.

---

19 The National Geographic Channel has a documentary called *Electronic Armageddon* specifically about the EMP threat to the grid. It can be purchased on their website. (https://shop.nationalgeographic.com/product/dvds/science/electronic-armageddon-dvd-r). For those who prefer a fictional setting, *Jericho* (CBS) and *Revolution* (NBC) are both of interest.

20 Graham, William R. (Chairman), et al. *Report of the Commission to Assess the Threat to the United States from Electromagnetic Pulse (EMP) Attack: Critical National Infrastructures*. (April 2008), p. 112.

What Challenges Face Our Town?

We can briefly broad-brush the challenges as follows:

- Long-term interruption of power
  - People will be without heat or air conditioning.
  - People will be without refrigeration.
  - People will be without the ability to perform basic things like cooking.
  - People will be without basic sanitation and, hence, at risk for diseases.
  - People may be without transportation immediately (damage to vehicle computer chips) or soon (lack of fuel).
  - Most, if not all, forms of communication will be disrupted.
- Long-term interruption of supply chain
  - Food delivery will stop.
  - Fuel delivery will stop.
  - Delivery of medicine and medical supplies to pharmacies and hospitals will stop.
  - Delivery of all products, parts and supplies will stop.
- Long-term interruption of essential services
  - Water service will stop.
  - Sewer service will stop.
  - Fire, EMS, and police will be unable to respond (for lack of fuel, personnel and communications).
  - Medical services will be severely disrupted or unavailable.
- Collapse of "rule of law" (temporary or permanent)
  - The police will not have the manpower, communications, or transportation to provide security for the community.
  - Desperate people will resort to looting, burglary, robbery, or any means necessary to get food and water.
  - It is unlikely that federal help will be "on the way" anytime soon.
  - Many local governments will quickly become ineffective.

- Starving refugees arriving from urban areas
  - Even if, miraculously, you live in a community that is prepared and has a plan to attack the above challenges, look to your nearest urban areas—refugees will soon be forced to flee the cities. Any plan for a town's survival will have to address how to humanely handle desperate refugees while protecting the town and maintaining law and order.
  - Town borders will have to be monitored and protected.
  - Town assets will have to be guarded from looters/criminals.

Individual Prepping Is Not Enough

FEMA-Recommended 72 Hours

If everybody took FEMA's advice and was prepared for basic emergencies, we would be much better off as a country. If there was a hurricane, flood, or local blackout, people having a basic level of preparedness will result in reduced casualties and better allow the government to devote resources where needed. Even in a "grid-down" scenario, everybody having an emergency plan and a 72-hour "bug out bag" (or "kit," in FEMA parlance) would save many lives— at least initially.

However, many people are woefully unprepared and have not even followed FEMA's most basic advice.[21] In terms of your town, every family that is not at least at this basic level of preparedness makes the town weaker. (More later on what a great opportunity this creates.)

Even One Year May Not Do It

Many people across the country fall into some category of "preppers." These are people who are prepared for an emergency well beyond the "FEMA 72-hour" standard and have given serious thought to various disaster and survival scenarios. But even if you are prepared to survive a year and have a basement full

---

21 http://www.ready.gov/ (accessed September 11, 2017).

of #10 cans, water and plenty of Sterno˚, long-term survival and security are tied to a community.

You can wait out the apocalypse in your basement (hoping you don't get into too many gunfights with looters—and that you win *every one* you do get into), emerging someday in the hopes that things are better (which they probably won't be). Or you can find others in your community now, who are interested in preparing the community for a long-term catastrophe and doing everything possible now, while we still have a grid and supply chain.

After the lights go out, it is too late to "prepare." All you can do at that point is react.

Communities Have a Greater Chance of Survival than Individuals

Collective Safety and Security

I know my limitations, and I know I cannot secure my family and our supplies in a "without rule of law" world. I have police and military training, and maybe I'm above average in terms of familiarity and training on security and firearms. But I am not Rambo, and this is not a movie or video game. Perhaps I can handle one armed intruder (if I'm awake and see him coming), but I can't handle an armed gang. I can't be patrolling 24/7. I have to sleep at some point. I am not fool enough to think I am "prepared" to provide meaningful security for my family. (Oh, I'm likely fool enough to try, but, when I fail, my wife, family, and pets will face the armed gang alone.)

So, it really doesn't matter how many guns and how many rounds of ammo you have. You need to have a realistic view of security, and you cannot do it alone. We'd be safer with a musket in a safe town than with an assault rifle in a "without rule of law" world. That may not be sexy, but it's the truth.

Safety and security are easier to achieve collectively than individually. If a town has an organized security force that is working shifts and guarding routes into the town, as well as guarding town assets (like water sources, critical buildings, and supplies), then maybe you can get a good night's sleep once in a while. Moreover, collective security will create an environment for other activities necessary for survival, such as food production. A nice field of crops will do you no good if you wake up one morning and it has been wiped out by looters. Security will allow you to establish medical facilities—which also is difficult in a "without rule of law" world. And security allows a small democratic government to continue.

Collective Resources

Our town has a reservoir, a river, and several streams and ponds. Our town has farmland. Our town has equipment. Our town has manpower. Our town has a great many resources that, if organized, protected, and used wisely, would increase the chances of survival for the families within our borders. Perhaps most importantly, our town has a democratic government that can organize, protect, and lead the people.

I can't start a farm. Our town can. I can't start a hospital. Our town can. I can't realistically protect my family. Our town can.

There is probably a reason that, back when we lived in caves, we had clans and tribes. Later, we had cities and towns. We always have lived together and survived together in communities.

Why on earth would anybody think this shouldn't be the case when the grid goes down?

Collective Skills

When I run out of commercial water filters and bleach someday, I have no idea how to purify water other than to boil it. However, somebody in my town probably knows how to build a reverse osmosis system, which could provide the town with potable water.[22]

I've dabbled in gardening, with all the Miracle-Gro®, pre-started tomato plants, and other modern stuff that Home Depot® sells, but I have never planted a field of crops from seeds. I have never milked a cow. I have only a general idea of which end of the chicken an egg comes from. However, somebody in my town is a farmer and has expertise in all these areas.

---

22 This will save many lives; people have always died of waterborne diseases in third-world countries—which we will be, if the grid goes down.

Somebody in my town is a doctor. Somebody in my town may know how to build a fish farm and raise fish. Somebody in my town may be a mechanic who can bypass EMP-fried circuits and get machines running. Somebody in my town can show us how to build solar ovens and wind energy devices. Somebody in my town was in the Peace Corps and taught third-world villages how and where to build latrines. And, God bless her, there is a little old lady in town somewhere who can teach us how to can and preserve vegetables.

We can teach each other the new (actually old and lost) skills that we need to survive. Not too many of us today have all these skills as individuals.

Beans, Bullets, and Bandages Are Not Enough

"Beans, bullets, and bandages" is an old military phrase meaning "logistics." In other words, you need to supply the troops engaging in the battle with the basic supplies they need to fight and survive. However, being able to do this assumes there is a supply line, at the end of which is a stockpile of stuff and/or a manufacturing capability.

In a long-term, grid-down scenario, eventually the supplies we have on hand will run out. Without a supply chain or manufacturing capability, when we're out, we're out. We can't just run to Cabela's® and buy another thousand rounds of ammo and more Mountain House® freeze-dried lasagna.

We need to start out with a long-term view. Obviously, the more we have on hand at the beginning, the more time we'll have to implement a long-term plan, but eventually we have to have sustainable permanent solutions. Since many problems (such as food production) may take significant time and effort—and many people could starve before the first crop is harvested—it is obviously a great advantage to have these plans (and resources) in place to bridge the gap *before* the grid goes down.

Afterward, you may have a great idea for a farm, but no seeds to plant.

So, assuming there will be a limited stockpile of "beans, bullets, and bandages" (supplies) at the beginning of an event, here are some questions that need to be answered in planning:

- How are we going to feed [X number of people] in the town?
- How are we going to equip/supply/train our security force?
- How are we going to provide potable water?
- How are we going to provide medical services?
- How are we going to provide safety, health, and sanitation measures?
- How are we going to maintain our government in the absence of state and federal resources (e.g., not every town has a court—and we will need one)?

A Civil Defense Program Can Work for Catastrophes, Small and Large

What if the world as we know it does not end? What if the federal government finally takes meaningful action to protect the grid? That's great. There will still be localized blackouts, floods, tornadoes, hurricanes, and so on. We should always "hope for the best, but prepare for the worst." A community that is prepared for the worst will be prepared for anything. Consequently, when a hurricane and resulting one-week blackout comes, oops—we were over prepared. Is that a bad thing?

A civil defense community preparedness plan can be modular. We should have the capability to do anything, from door-to-door health and welfare checks during a few-day-long power outage[23] to full-scale catastrophe response, if terrorists take down the grid with an EMP or cyber strike.

Unprepared Communities Will Be Forced to React after the Fact—A Difficult Proposition at Best

If the grid goes down right now, how many local governments have thought about what they would do? The federal, state, and local governments do

---

23 One possibility for a civil defense organization to consider is working with the local authorities to set up a Community Emergency Response Team (CERT). More information is available at: http://www.fema.gov/community-emergency-response-teams (accessed August 28, 2017).

"tabletop" drills—or even actual drills—on typical disaster response scenarios (such as hurricanes). I've been involved in a few of these, and it seems that in the "game" there are always outside resources and agencies available. I don't ever recall being involved in any drill where the premise was "your town is totally screwed and all alone."

Shouldn't each town have a drill where the scenario is that the power goes off, all outside communications are cut off, and nobody from the outside (state or federal) can be reached? I doubt there are many towns that have done this.

In August 2012, Congressman Roscoe Bartlett (who has been instrumental in raising the nation's awareness of EMP threats and attempting to spur the federal government into action to address the threats), along with members of Congress Yvette D. Clarke, Trent Franks and Hank Johnson, introduced a resolution.[24] The House failed to act on the resolution.

The proposed resolution:

(1) encourages every community to develop its own "civil defense program" working with citizens, leaders, and institutions, ranging from local fire halls, schools, and faith-based organizations, to create sustainable local infrastructure and planning capacity, so that it might mitigate high-impact scenarios and be better prepared to survive and recover from these worst-case disaster scenarios and be better able to affordably and sustainably meet the needs of the community in times of peace and tranquility;

(2) encourages every citizen to develop an individual emergency plan to prepare for the absence of government assistance for extended periods;

(3) encourages each local community to foster the capability of providing at least 20 percent of its own critical needs, such as local power generation, food, and water, while protecting local infrastructure whenever possible from the threats that threaten centralized infrastructure; and to do so with the urgency and importance inherent in an all-of-nation civil defense program developed by citizens and their local communities; and

---

24 The proposed resolution is included in its entirety as Appendix 1.

(4) encourages state governments and federal agencies to support the ability of local communities to become stronger, self-reliant, and better able to assist neighboring communities in times of great need.

I think this resolution speaks for itself, and it is unfortunate that it didn't pass. However, a good idea does not need to pass Congress to be a good idea.

Unfortunately, in communities that do not create a "civil defense program" as described in the resolution, many people will die and many valuable resources will be looted before such a structure can be created from scratch. Those communities and the people in them will be behind the survival eight ball.

Two

A Civil Defense Community
Survival Plan in Action

America

Everybody remembers where they were when the lights went off. I was in math class, which was not my favorite. I never told anybody this, but I was glad at first when the lights went out during math. I was staring at the American flag in the corner while the teacher was talking, and suddenly all the lights went off. Just like that. After a while, the principal came to the classroom and whispered outside in the hall to my teacher. Kids can always tell when something is wrong, and I heard some of the girls cry a little.

A little while later, some high school kids came to my school, and each of them took a group of us kids from a list. They said they were going to walk us all home, because the buses were not working. All the kids on the list with me were from my same neighborhood. The high school kids who came for us were all wearing those orange vests that the police wear when they direct traffic.

The girl who walked my group home said her name was Jennifer. She does not live far from my street. She told us not to be scared, but the power was out, and it was her job to take us home. She said she had to make sure that somebody from our family was there, or a next door neighbor; otherwise, we would stay with her until somebody from our family came home.

It seemed really quiet on the walk home, and I noticed some cars in the middle of the street. It dawned on me after a while that there were no cars driving down the roads. Even on Main Street, when we crossed it, there were no cars driving. I saw a few people with the hoods of their cars up, looking at the engines.

My mom and dad both worked in the city. Nobody was home at my house, so I stayed with Jennifer and helped her get the other kids home. I was the oldest kid in my group—most of them were in the lower grades—so I helped get the kids to their houses and turn them over to their parents. A few whose parents weren't home stayed with neighbors. Jennifer told me that my parents might not be home today, because they would probably have to walk home from work, so I should come with her. She left a note on my front door for my parents that I was OK and with her.

Jennifer's dad was home when we got to her house. When I told him my name, he said that he knows my mom and dad from Civil Defense. My mom and dad always used to go to Civil Defense meetings, and sometimes they marched in the parades with the Civil Defense people. In the summer, Civil Defense has bike contests for the kids, where we have to deliver secret messages on our bikes to different places. The kids who do the best in the contests used to win a new bike! The bike contests started before the lights went out, but they still do them now. Since there are no more new bikes, we win other prizes now. It's still a lot of fun.

Jennifer's dad was in his Civil Defense militia uniform when we got there. He said that he had to report to the police station, because with the power out, the police would need the militia's help. The militia's job is to help the police protect the town. You see, Civil Defense had all these different groups, like the militia, a medical group, a food group, a water group, and some others. Even some of the high school kids, like Jennifer, were in Civil Defense; their first job was to take care of the younger kids and get us home safely.

Now I know why they did all that stuff in Civil Defense. When the power went out, the first thing they wanted to do was get all the kids home to their families—or find someplace for them to stay, if their parents hadn't made it home yet. The second thing they wanted to do was get all the families back together. The people in Civil Defense tell everyone who works in the city to have "get-home bags" at work or in their cars. My mom and dad took the bus to work, but they both had get-home bags in their offices. They had every-thing they needed to walk home from work in those bags.

My dad was a lawyer, but after the lights went out, the town made him the judge. It is a really important job. The town never had a court before the lights went out, but now there is a court. As the judge, my dad solves all kinds of problems. For example, if the town needs to use somebody's land to plant crops, they will talk with the owner to work it out. If they can't, they go before my dad, and he says what needs to happen. His word is final. Maybe the town will have to pay the owner some food or supplies to use the land. My dad says he likes it when he can make everybody happy, but sometimes he can't. There are other lawyers called mediators, who my dad sends out to solve problems in the town. If they can't solve the problem between the people, then the people come to my dad, and he listens and then tells them what has to happen.

Once, my dad had to banish somebody out of the town. It was a guy who broke into a house and stole food from his neighbors. That is one of the worst crimes. Stealing can be punishable by banishment from the town for-ever. They let his family give him a bag with water and other things, and then the militia brought him to the border and told him to start walking and never come back. It was big news in the town, but I bet nobody will steal from their neighbors again. We had to talk about it at school. The kids asked me a lot of questions, because they know my dad's the judge. I told them what my dad told me: Everybody has to obey the law, so we will all survive. Anytime you break a law, you hurt the town. And if people don't like a law, they can change it at the elections.

My mom used to work at the hospital in the city. She's a nurse. She didn't come home for a few days after the lights went out, but then the hospital closed, and all the doctors and nurses had to leave. My mom said the city is no longer safe, and the police are gone. When my mom and dad thought I was asleep one night, I heard her telling him about her walk home. She had to hide almost the whole way home and almost didn't make it. Now my mom works in the hospital in town. We actually didn't have a hospital before the blackout, but we do now. It was an office building before, but the town took it over as a hospital. We have doctors, nurses, dentists and even a veterinarian.

My dad says that someday, if the owner of the building comes, the town will pay him rent for the building that is now the hospital. My dad says that we always have to respect property, but sometimes the town has to come first. Anybody has the right to go to my dad if they don't agree with something the town does. My dad will even give them a lawyer, if they want one. But after they talk, and the town's lawyer talks, my dad decides what will happen, and that is it.

Back to my mom—she used to go to Civil Defense meetings with the doctors and nurses before the lights went out, and they decided that the town would need a hospital if anything bad ever happened. They raised money and stored as many supplies as they could. We had a hospital right away when the lights went out.

My uncle is a captain in the militia. He used to be a police officer in another town, but he said that town no longer exists. When the lights went out, Civil Defense made him a captain. He is in charge of several roads into town that have to be guarded 24 hours a day. When refugees come, the militia has to either turn them away or escort them to the other side of town and let them continue on their way. Lots of people tried to come here the first year, but the town said that we couldn't take them. We didn't have enough food for us, much less all the people who left the city. We always give them water, because we have plenty of water; and sometimes our medics will check them out, but we can't usually spare much medicine.

Now there are not as many refugees coming to the gates on our roads as there used to be. My dad told me that a lot of people outside of our town died from starvation and diseases. Others might have found other places to live. But people from the outside try to sneak in all the time to steal from us. The militia is always looking for people trying to sneak in, and also there is always somebody from the militia in every neighborhood all the time to keep us safe. Nobody is allowed on the street after dark except the militia, unless it is an emergency. If you have to go out after dark for an emergency, you have to wear an orange vest, so they will know you are from town.

I want to be in the militia like my uncle someday. He's my hero. But my dad and mom are also my heroes. Every role in the town is important. There is even this crazy guy in town, who used to talk about starting a fish farm during the Civil Defense meetings before the power went out. We have a river that runs through the town, and this guy wanted to plan a fish farm. People thought he was nuts, but when the lights went out, they listened to him. Now, we have fish to eat sometimes, because of this guy. He is a town hero now, and they say he is one of the ones who saved us with food. Next year, he says there will be even more fish.

We learned in school that the food people in Civil Defense are heroes, because they saved all of us. We learned that millions of people starved after the lights went out, but in our town, not one person ever starved to death. Sure, we were all hungry the first year and had to eat a lot of gross food, but we all at least got enough food to keep us alive. They say in school that it was a miracle we all lived—but a miracle made by people. All of us have to work on the farms during the harvest and maybe one day a week during the summer. Even my dad goes. He says it is good for all the people to see him and the first selectman and the police chief weeding and tending to the crops with everybody else. My uncle told me that my dad leads by example.

In school we learned that the first selectman is the head of the town. The people elect who they want as the first selectman. It was that way before the lights went out, and it is still that way. The three top leaders in town are the first selectman, the police chief, and the judge—my dad. But there are also other important people, like the chief doctor, the chief mechanic, and the chief farmer, who give advice to the first selectman.

After the lights went out, there were new laws passed in the town. Here's one: You are not allowed to throw away any clothes, blankets, or cloth. If you have old clothes that are worn out or don't fit, you give them to Civil Defense. There are these ladies who take all the cloth and make new clothes and blankets. They are really good. They make the militia uniforms now, and also blankets for the winter. The uniforms look like you bought them in a store. Some of the older kids work with them now, to learn how to make clothes and dye cloth.

My role right now is a messenger. All kids get a role when they are 12 now. The kids who are messengers get to wear a uniform, which I like, and we deliver messages on our bikes from the militia posts to the either the police station, a house, or a radio relay. You have to know all the streets and shortcuts, and it is important that every message gets delivered. A message can save a life. Some of the kids get to use a canoe to deliver messages along the river, but only in good weather. Otherwise, they have to use a bike, which takes longer. Now we have school every other day, and when we are not in school, we do our roles.

We only have a few radios in town, so there are not enough for every militia post. All of the radios from before the lights went out won't work anymore, but Civil Defense had a few radios stored in metal boxes that kept those radios safe. The mechanics got three generators running—one for the police station, one for the water plant, and one for the hospital—but fuel is scarce, so the police station does not run their generator all the time. But they can charge up the batteries for the radios, and messengers bring the charged batteries out to the relays and bring the old ones back. That can be a long ride on a bike, but a battery can save lives.

Some kids get other roles. My friend works on the fish farm, and one of the girls in my class helps take care of the horses. The horses are important to the town, because we use them to help plow and pull supply carts. The mechanics got a few of the old tractors working for the farms, but fuel is scarce. A lot of people wanted to eat the horses the first year, because we were so hungry, but the town said no. The horses could help us make a lot more food in the farms. I'm glad, because I like horses, and I really don't want to eat one.

At first, the mechanics got some vehicles working, but because fuel is scarce, the hospital uses one van for an ambulance, and the police use one van in case they have to get the militia's emergency team to a gate or somewhere fast. That's about it for vehicles now, except the tractors. We use some of the dead cars now to dry fruits and vegetables for the winter. The mechanics used the metal from some of the other cars, along with old hot water heaters from people's basements, and made wood stoves for the houses.

Sometimes, the town sends people out to other towns, but it is very dangerous once you leave the border, and we have to send a squad of militia with them. Most of the other towns are in a lot of trouble, and we try to help them by telling them how we have things set up here. We were the only town around here with Civil Defense before the lights went out. Now the other towns wish they had Civil Defense. They always want food from us, but we don't have enough yet. We are hoping that after the next harvest, we may have enough food to trade some for fuel.

Once, when I delivered a message to the police station, I talked to one of the guys who listens to the shortwave radio. Civil Defense had the radio in the metal box before the lights went out, so it still works. The guy told me that I am very lucky to live in this town. Messengers, police, and the militia all have an American flag on their uniforms. The shortwave guy pointed to the flag on my shoulder and told me that we are all that's left of America, as far as he can tell.

Next year, my class will start internships. We will work some at the hospital, at the farms, with the militia, with the water plant, at the fish farm, with the mechanics, and with the government. Every kid has to spend time in each area, so that we learn that all jobs in town are important. That is also where we start to decide with our parents and teachers what job we are going to train for. When we turn 18, we will start our jobs and can vote in the elections. My mom and dad say that voting is the most important thing we do. It is important to choose good people to lead us.

I'm hoping my uncle will talk to my dad about letting me train for the militia, because I really want to help protect the town and America when I grow up.

Three

SOME KEY CONSIDERATIONS FOR A CIVIL DEFENSE ORGANIZATION

The fictional town in the previous chapter had a civil defense organization in place prior to the national catastrophe and had planned out several critical issues ahead of time, such as security, food, water, and even the need for a hospital and a court, which did not exist prior to the event. Presumably, they had been at least somewhat successful in their activities to promote family and community preparedness, and this paid off when the power grid went down. They executed their plans, instead of having to react to every emergency from scratch, which would overwhelm any local government in a catastrophe.

They obviously were not fully successful, because "we were all hungry the first year and had to eat a lot of gross food, but we all at least got enough food to keep us alive." Also, "fuel is scarce," and "we only have a few radios in town." So, while perhaps they did not convince every family in town to have a one-year supply of food stored, somehow failed on the fuel planning, and should have squirrelled a few more two-way radios onto their Faraday cages,[25] they had done enough prepping to enable the town to survive. The towns around them did not fare as well.

They did not need to be perfect (and probably no town ever will be), but they did appear to do a good job of covering some key concerns. Let's look at a few of the items that the narrator observed:

---

25 Named for Michael Faraday, a 19th century scientist, a Faraday cage is a structure that can protect its contents from static electric fields and electromagnetic radiation by distributing the energy around the exterior of the cage.

1. *Public Service and Awareness Activities prior to the Event*
   - The Civil Defense organization had made itself part of the town's culture. They marched in the parades and held bike races for the kids in town (which actually doubled as a training event).
   - The Civil Defense organization held meetings and brainstormed about what would be needed ahead of time (e.g., the hospital and the fish farm).
   - The Civil Defense organization raised money and obtained supplies, including medical supplies and radios stored in Faraday cages.

2. *When the Event Happened, People Knew What to Do*
   - The schools knew how to get the kids home (e.g., Jennifer's group of high school kids in the Civil Defense system).
   - Jennifer's father knew that the militia needed to report to the police station.

3. *Helping Families to Get Back Together Quickly*
   - Knowing that your people's first priority will be the safety of their families (and they are not going to be able to focus on Civil Defense tasks until they know their families are safe), this is Job 1 for the Civil Defense. I don't know how many communities out there have a plan to get the kids home from school after an EMP or solar flare (probably none), but imagine the chaos if transportation is disrupted, parents are stuck at their jobs, and kids are stuck at their schools. This town had a plan for this scenario.
   - The Civil Defense organization had "get-home bag" awareness for people who worked out of town.
   - If the parents weren't home, the kids were placed with neighbors or with a Civil Defense family, and a note was left for the parents.

4. *Long-Term Solutions*
   - Wood-burning stoves for homes were fabricated from existing materials (old hot water heaters and metal from cars).
   - The town had a method for manufacturing clothes and blankets.

- The entire town was involved in the food production effort.
- The education system included training the children in needed skills.
- There was an organized, trained militia to protect the town from looters and crime, and to manage refugees.
- The town established a court (with criminal and civil capabilities) and established a dispute resolution process.
- The town was able to prioritize and effectively use its critical resources for the long-term good (priority for fuel, use of the few horses, etc.).
- The town maintained democracy.
- Perhaps most importantly, a child in the town seemed to look forward to the future—and actually had a future.

Here is a list of some of the key areas to think about. This is not comprehensive—just the general buckets. Every community is unique and has different resources and different challenges. But this is a good starting checklist to make sure that the most essential functions are covered.

Preparedness Activities Before the Event

How prepared is the average family in town? What can be done to increase awareness on preparedness prior to an event? Is there an active and organized Civil Defense group? Is there a plan for a "worst-case scenario" (loss of grid nationwide, loss of communications and supply chain)? Is anybody taking action to prepare the town? There is a great opportunity here for a Civil Defense group to advocate and educate the townspeople on the FEMA preparedness checklist.[26] If more people in town are *at least* this prepared, the town will have made progress. Also, it will get the Civil Defense group's name out there as a player and can help build credibility and generate interest in prepping. Consider having the Civil Defense organization become involved in starting a

---

26 http://www.ready.gov/sites/default/files/documents/files/checklist3.pdf (accessed August 1, 2017).

Community Emergency Response Team (CERT).[27] Remember, emergencies are "come as you are." The goals of a Civil Defense group should be to increase individual and family preparedness *as well as* overall town preparedness.

Activation

The town leaders and Civil Defense leaders need to be able to recognize the signs that this is not a "routine local power outage" and activate the Civil Defense system. Assume that communications will be disrupted. How will the Civil Defense be activated, and what do the various members do initially?

Plan for Family Reunification

How will kids be reunited with their parents, if the event happens during a school day? How will citizens get home, if they work outside of the town or in a neighboring city?

Security and Community Protection

Most towns will need a militia to supplement the police. In small towns with no police force, the militia may be all they have. Even if a town has a police force, it will not have enough people. Some towns may have only two patrol officers and a sergeant on a shift (or even less). Looting can start quickly, and you can't "unloot" what is lost.

Communications

If electronics, power, and phones (and possibly vehicles) are affected, what are the contingency plans for communications? Worst-case scenario for

---

27 http://www.fema.gov/community-emergency-response-teams (accessed August 1, 2017).

communications might be an EMP/solar flare. What would you do then? (And what should be done before then?)

Food

There is a lot to think about here; if the supply chain goes down, all you have to work with is whatever individual people (and perhaps the Civil Defense organization) have stored—and, perhaps, an unlooted grocery store, if you have one in town. What could be done quickly after the power goes out to preserve perishable food? What food does your town produce now? What would need to be done if you had to produce food for the town's population? How can you bridge the gap between now and the harvest?

Water

Access to potable water is necessary for life and to prevent waterborne diseases. You will have enough problems without adding widespread waterborne disease outbreaks. Does the town have water sources and the means to purify and transport water in a "grid-down" scenario? If it will take a while to get a water purification operation running, what can be done in the meantime?

Shelter and Safety

Although people may have houses, most houses are dependent on electricity for heat, lighting, and cooking. In the winter especially, people are going to be cold and may be apt to do dangerous things to stay warm. Add this to a decreased ability of the fire department to respond (lack of communications, lack of fuel, and possible EMP damage to equipment), and the danger of house fires is tremendous. Lack of smoke detectors will add to the fire risk. Thought must be given to safe ways to cook, safe use of lighting (e.g., solar garden lights, candles and oil lamps), and ways for people to keep warm. Most households are not equipped to survive through a cold winter without power, and not everyone in town has an extreme-cold sleeping bag. In the long run, many (or all) houses may need to be retrofitted with safe wood fireplaces or wood-burning stoves, using existing materials.

Sanitation

This goes hand in hand with water. Failure of sewer systems can lead to contamination of water sources and will be a major danger in terms of the spread of disease. Does every family have instructions on how and where to build an outdoor latrine? If not, the town is at risk. Also, the garbage truck isn't coming anymore. What is the plan for disposal of garbage? If there is no plan, expect it to be dumped inappropriately, which can lead to rodents, disease and other problems.

Medical

What medical facilities, if any, does the town already have? What additional facilities will be needed? What medical personnel live in town and might be available during an emergency? How can the town bridge the gaps, if there are not sufficient medical staff available (doctors, nurses, paramedics, etc.)? What equipment and supplies are critical? What pharmacies are in town? (They will be among the first targets for looters.)

Power and Fuel

There is uncertainty about the effects of an EMP or solar flare on equipment such as vehicles and generators. Best-case scenario is that the equipment works, but you still will only have whatever fuel is available in town. Worst-case scenario is that none of the equipment that has electrical components and circuitry works. Assume the worst for planning. Can the town get some generators working again, if they are affected? How? If fuel supplies cease, how much fuel will be available, and how would it be rationed? What are the most important needs for fuel/power, if it is limited? For the long term, thought should be given to alternative power sources, such as wind and solar, and protecting them from an EMP/solar flare.

Maintain Democracy

If there is not a court in your community, it is something important to think about. Our government has a system of checks and balances among the executive, legislative, and judicial branches. This prevents one person, or one branch of the government, from having too much power. If the town decides that they need to do X, which affects a citizen or his or her property, to whom can the aggrieved citizen appeal? Establishing a court and appointing a judge (who can agree with the town's action, overrule a town action, or order remedies) will go a long way to ensure that democracy is maintained—and that the citizens have their voices heard. Also, crimes are still going to happen. Trial and punishment (e.g., the banishment of a citizen in the fictional town) are best dispensed by a court, not a police chief or mayor. Conduct *regular, scheduled elections*. This should go without saying, but let me say it. Elections by the people are the cornerstone of our democracy. It is critical that scheduled elections be conducted, and that transfer of power is orderly and efficient.

It appears to be a daunting list, and perhaps no plans yet exist in your town for a "worst-case scenario." A few people can change this. A Civil Defense organization can start with just a small group of people who have an interest in preparing their community. How do you eat an elephant? One bite at a time.

Four

As a Nonprofit

The ideal approach is to establish an active nonprofit civil defense organization that is accepted by the town in disaster planning. It should also have credibility with the town and public, on par with the fire department and volunteer ambulance service. The organization would have active groups of volunteers planning, educating and marshaling knowledge and resources for all of the critical areas:

- Planning group
- Medical group
- Security (militia) group
- Food group
- Water group
- Safety, health, and sanitation group
- Legal group (court and democracy)
- Communications group
- Alternative power, equipment, and skills group
- Finance (fundraising) and community outreach group

"In general, providing relief to victims of a disaster is a charitable activity because it aims to relieve human suffering—charity in its most basic form."[28]

---

28 U.S. Internal Revenue Service, *Disaster Relief: Standards for Charities that Provide Relief to Individuals.* https://www.irs.gov/charities-non-profits/charitable-organizations/

Before an event, the organization would engage in activities to educate the town's citizens on emergency preparedness and self-reliance—a § 501(c)(3) tax-exempt "educational" purpose. It would also engage in activities to plan and obtain knowledge and resources to assist the town in providing disaster relief to the town's citizens in a worst-case scenario catastrophe—a § 501(c)(3) tax-exempt charitable purpose.

In the event of a catastrophe and activation of the civil defense organization, the organization will be able to provide disaster relief and provide the town additional resources and capabilities for the safety and welfare of its citizens that the town would not have had—a § 501(c)(3) tax-exempt charitable purpose.

It is also possible that the organization may meet the § 501(c)(3) tax-exempt purpose of "lessening the burdens of government." However, the test for this is quite stringent so the particular functions of the organization and its relationship with the municipality must be studied to make sure the facts and circumstances would pass IRS review.[29]

It is important to make sure that the organizational documents satisfy the requirements in your state for a nonprofit and also meet the IRS test for a § 501(c)(3) tax-exempt organization.[30] Although you do not need a lawyer to start a nonprofit, there are legal and reporting requirements involved in creating, incorporating, and running a nonprofit, so it is advisable to seek legal advice to make sure you meet all the requirements.

The IRS describes the § 501(c)(3) organization test as follows:

---

disaster-relief-standards-for-charities-that-provide-relief-to-individuals (accessed September 11, 2017).

29 According to the IRS: "A determination of whether an organization is lessening the burdens of government requires consideration of whether the organization's activities are ones that a government unit considers to be its burden, and whether such activities actually lessen that burden, based on all the facts and circumstances. *See* Rev. Rul. 85-1 (organization that assists a county's law enforcement agencies in policing illegal narcotics traffic lessens burdens of government); Rev. Rul. 85-2 (organization that provides legal counsel and training to volunteers who serve as guardians *ad litum* in a juvenile court dependency program lessens the burdens of government.)" http://www.irs.gov/irb/2011-16_IRB/ar07.html (accessed August 2, 2017).

30 See http://www.irs.gov/pub/irs-tege/eotopicd04.pdf (accessed August 2, 2017) for a good description of the requirements.

An organization is organized exclusively for one or more § 501(c)(3) exempt purposes only if its creating document:

- Limits the purposes of such organizations to one or more exempt purposes;
- Does not expressly empower the organization to engage, other than as an insubstantial part of its activities, in activities which in themselves are not in furtherance of one or more exempt purposes; and
- Permanently dedicates the organization's assets to § 501(c)(3) purposes on dissolution.

Your organizational documents will need to meet these criteria if you intend to be a § 501(c)(3) tax-exempt organization.

§ 501(c)(3) Organization vs. § 501(c)(4) Organization

Another nonprofit structure is a § 501(c)(4) organization. Here are some of the key differences:

§ 501(c)(3)	§ 501(c)(4)
<ul><li>Either a public charity, private foundation, or private operating foundation with open membership</li><li>Donations are tax deductible</li><li>May not participate in political campaigns</li><li>Extreme limits on lobbying and supporting legislation</li></ul>	<ul><li>Civic leagues or associations operated exclusively for the promotion of social welfare or local associations of employees with limited membership</li><li>Donations are not tax deductible</li><li>Can participate in political campaigns</li><li>May engage in unlimited lobbying, as long as it pertains to the organization's mission</li></ul>

The advantage of a donor being able to make tax deductible donations to the organization is an important feature of the § 501(c)(3) structure. Also, and of critical importance: displaying a political agenda will not be in the best interests of an organization that you would like the entire town to accept. You need both the pro- and the anti-[pick your issue] people to all believe in the survival of the town, and there is no value in alienating any citizens over political issues. Therefore, the § 501(c)(3) structure is the best option for a nonprofit civil defense organization.

To obtain tax-exempt status under Section 501(c)(3) of the Internal Revenue Code, an organization must file a Form 1023 with the IRS. The wait time for IRS approval can be as long as one year. The Form 1023 looks simple, but it is easy to make mistakes and the pitfalls are many. It is best to consult a knowledgeable attorney for assistance when filing the organization's creating documents and IRS documents.

As an Informal Group, Club or Unincorporated Association

It is not advisable to operate without a formal legal structure. The dangers of operating as an informal group, club or unincorporated association are:

a) Individuals may be personally liable for the obligations, actions and liabilities of the group.
b) Donors, foundations, governmental agencies, and others will require incorporation and eventual tax-exempt status.
c) Third parties may give more credence to a formally structured organization.
d) The applicable state statute will generally provide many default governance provisions that don't exist if the organization is not incorporated.

If your thought is to eventually end up as a fairly large, organized, and credible nonprofit, it would be advantageous to structure your initial mission statement, charter, and Bylaws with this goal in mind. In other words, it would be a good idea to start from the outset with the § 501(c)(3) tax-exempt purposes and structure your activities around these purposes—which happen to be perfect for community prepping and civil defense.

How to Start

Start with two preppers from the same town, a pot of coffee, and this book. Then find a few more people in your town to get involved. Each new person in your "discussion circle" will possibly know other people in town. Everybody does not have to be a "card-carrying prepper." You want anybody interested in the town's disaster preparedness. People like to be consulted on their areas of expertise, so try something like this:

> "Hey, Joe, some friends of mine and I are interested in starting a civil defense group to help the town out if there were ever a major disaster, like a long-term power outage. Since you're on the volunteer fire department, I thought you might have some ideas. Can you come over Thursday night and talk with us?"

The worst thing that can happen is, Joe comes over, is not interested in joining you, but gives you some great insight into the town's emergency response capabilities and plans and the names of people in the town who are involved in emergency preparedness. Everything you can learn is useful. And getting some people involved early on who are part of the town's emergency preparedness system will be a huge coup in terms of other contacts, information, and having insiders talk up the benefits of the organization with others you want to persuade. Police, fire department, EMS, and town employees are all good prospects.

Your initial group should agree on a mission statement. Appendix 2 has some samples you can use as starting points to begin building a civil defense organization. You need a few people who are willing to devote some time and effort to this—it's not going to build itself.

Starting to Research and Build a Plan

Good places to start are the most recent census data on your town, information from the town's website, and maps (street, topographic, and satellite). Start to build a "broad brush" profile of the town:

<u>Town Y</u>
Population: 10,292 (as of the 2010 census)
Total households: 4086 (as of the 2010 census)
Total area: 25.0 square miles
Police department: 12 officers (sergeant and below)
Firehouses: 3 (volunteer)
EMS: Volunteer ambulance
Hospitals: None
Walk-in medical: None
Major water sources:

- White River
- Blue Reservoir
- Several ponds and streams

Gas stations: 3
Grocery stores: 1 large, 1 small
Pharmacies: 2
Roads crossing town border: 24

1. Case Street [Borders Town G]
2. North Town Y Road (RT 123) [Borders Town B]
3. Wright Road [Borders Town B]
4. Frey Road [Borders Town N]
5. Etc., etc.

Look at the geography of the town and start to think about the challenges of a long-term catastrophe outlined in Chapter 1. What are the water sources (rivers, streams, and lakes)? What is upstream from these water sources that could contaminate them, if the grid goes down? How many roads cross the border with neighboring towns? Are there existing farms that produce food? Who owns them, and what do they produce? What businesses in town are critical and would need immediate protection from looting (grocery stores, gas stations, pharmacies, sporting goods stores, etc.)?

As you get more people involved in thinking about preparedness, you can begin to break into work groups to look in more detail at the most critical areas. These will later become more formal sections.[31]

    i.   **Planning Work Group [Section]**
        a.   Gathering information and beginning to outline plans
    ii. **Operations Work Group [Section]**
        a.   Medical
        b.   Security (militia)
        c.   Communications
        d.   Safety, health, and sanitation
        e.   Legal/democracy
    iii. **Logistics Work Group [Section]**
        a.   Food
        b.   Water
        c.   Alternative power, equipment, and skills
    iv. **Finance and Community Outreach Work Group [Section]**
        a.   Raising funds for the organizations activities
        b.   Getting the word out to the community on emergency preparedness

More can be added later. Start with gathering information and thinking about the basic needs such as security, food, water, shelter, and medical care.

Pitching the Plan

The most knowledgeable and enthusiastic person in your group may be the guy who has lived "off-grid" for 15 years, dresses in homemade clothes, and gave up shaving before your oldest child was born. However, perhaps he is not the best front man to talk with the mayor. Your group should think immediately about credibility and first impressions. A business owner or lawyer in a suit might make a better first impression on the mayor than somebody who

---

31 This structure is based on the model for an Incident Command System (ICS) structure used by emergency management organizations.

resembles the Unabomber. If you have a police sergeant or fire lieutenant in your group, one of them would be a credible spokesperson for your group to begin a dialog with town officials. Your spokesperson can try something like this:

> "Mr. Mayor, we are a group of town residents forming a nonprofit organization. Our mission would be educating the public on emergency preparedness and providing resources to the town in the event of a disaster. We'd like to come in and talk with you about how we believe we can help."

There are two target audiences for the civil defense organization: the town government and the townspeople. Your initial planning and outreach strategy should be how to best approach these two groups. Every town government is different, with different personalities and different attitudes about preparedness. Some are open-minded. Some, not so much.

You may luck out and get some interest right away from some emergency management people in your town's government, and they can help you to pitch the plan. If it is smooth sailing, great.

If you encounter skepticism or indifference from the town government, don't be discouraged. Stay professional, and keep the door open. Keep working on it. (If the grid goes down, they will be glad you are there.) If you can't get the mayor, continue to try to get the police, fire, and EMS involved—these groups tend to be more in tune with the concept of emergency preparedness.

You want to plan activities to build public support and to show that the civil defense group is an important player in town preparedness. Use uncontroversial literature. For example, have a campaign to educate the public on the importance of the FEMA preparedness plan for families (www.ready.gov). You can even order copies of the publications from the government, or download and print copies. If your town already has some emergency preparedness literature, use that also.

Nobody from the town government can squawk if you are running around distributing federal government (and town) literature on readiness—and you are accomplishing your mission of educating the public on emergency preparedness! Continue to build community support. The town government will have to warm up to you eventually, if you are doing good work.

One way to get a foot in the door is for the organization to work with the town on setting up a Community Emergency Response Team (CERT).[32] That could be one aspect of the civil defense organization's activities and a good way to get other townspeople involved.

The public education campaign is also a way to find other people interested in participating in the organization.

---

32 http://www.fema.gov/community-emergency-response-teams (accessed August 2, 2017).

Five

The Security Force (Militia)

The security force (militia)[33] is critical to the community in a long-term catastrophe. Nothing else may matter if the town does not have security, law, and order.

Today, the term "militia" may carry some unfortunate connotations for some people. While we all learned that the militia in 1775 at the battles of Lexington and Concord were heroes in the founding of our country, today that isn't necessarily the image that comes to mind when we hear the word. Just be aware of this, and that the term "security force" or "town guard" may be more palatable to some. That's fine. It's not productive to argue over a name at first. If "security force" draws more support than "militia," so be it for now. Someday, when you've established credibility with the town, they will be proud of their "militia" and will call it that.

If you think about why some people find the term "militia" scary, but do not find the term "National Guard" scary, a key difference is instructive here: the National Guard is activated, deployed, directed and deactivated by the governor of a state. As for the word "militia", there have been lots of groups in the news that call themselves militias. Usually, they are portrayed in the media as "gun nuts" (or worse) that are not under government control. That's what makes the word scary to many people. The model proposed here more closely

---

33 The terms "security force" and "militia" are used interchangeably here.

resembles a town-scale "National Guard." The town government would activate, deploy, direct and deactivate this security force in an emergency.[34]

If your town has an existing police department, in an emergency, the security force (militia) would report to the police chief and supplement the existing police department. The most efficient way to work is to cooperatively plan and train with the police department before an event.

If your town's police department is initially not interested in joint planning or training, this should not dissuade the civil defense organization from preparing. If the grid goes down, attitudes are likely to change quickly, and needed help is not likely to be refused. In this instance, it is wise to try to develop as cordial a relationship as possible and keep the lines of communication open. The security force is a town asset, and eventually everybody should see this, if the civil defense organization is effective in its preparedness education mission.

If your town does not have an existing police force, in an emergency, the security force (militia) would report to the head elected official (mayor, town manager, first selectman) or that person's designee, such as the head of emergency management. The civil defense organization will want to plan and train with those officials. In this case, the security force (militia) may be the only organized defense and law and order asset the town has.

Becoming an integrated part of the town's emergency management structure is a strategic goal for the entire civil defense organization.

Sample Security Force (Militia) Qualifications

Although anybody in town, regardless of physical condition or past history, can play important roles in the civil defense organization, not everyone is qualified or has what it takes to serve on the security force.

The members of the security force must be willing and able to endure harsh conditions and heavy physical activity for long periods of time. They

---

34 Another key difference is, of course, budget. The state has a budget for the National Guard but the town does not. In this model, the civil defense organization would provide whatever funding and resources that are needed, but the town government would activate, deploy, direct and deactivate the militia.

will likely have to work long shifts, almost entirely outdoors, in every weather condition that your region can throw at them. They will have to do this even when they are cold, wet, sick, or starving. If called to service, it will not be a glamorous job. It's not for everyone.

The members of the security force must all be professional, of high moral character, and must gain the trust and respect of the townspeople and the town government. There is no room for even one bad apple. The civil defense organization needs to set high standards for recruitment and must not be shy about weeding out any potential problems before they become real problems. There is little room for error.

In an emergency, the members of the security force may be the face of the town government to many people, especially to people in remote areas. The medic in a militia squad may be the primary medical resource for a remote area of town, if transportation to the hospital is an issue. The security force may be the main source of news and information for some townspeople as well as the best source of information for the town government on conditions and needs in remote areas. In short, the security force must develop the level of trust and respect that soldiers, police, and fire departments have.

The members of the security force are likely going to have to provide most, if not all, of their own uniforms and equipment, and this can be a substantial expense.[35] In addition, they will have to be willing to devote substantial time to training.

An effective security force must be well-trained, well-equipped, well-regulated, and well-led. To that end, a lot of thought and effort will need to go into crafting qualifications, standards, and procedures for the security force.

Below are some suggested minimum requirements. If your organization is actively working with the town police on the security aspect of the civil defense plan, the police department should concur with the qualifications and requirements. If not, try to fashion the requirements so that Security Force members would at least meet the minimum requirements for an applicant for the town police department.

---

35 Check with the IRS and a qualified tax advisor for rules on deductions for uniforms and unreimbursed expenses incurred while performing charitable work.

RECRUITMENT QUALIFICATIONS

__ Must meet all requirements for a volunteer in the [Town Y] Civil Defense Corp.

__ Must be at least 21 years old.

__ Must have a high school diploma or GED.

__ Must pass a criminal background check.

__ Must be physically and mentally capable of performing the required tasks.

   __ Must provide a fitness certification from a medical doctor.

   __ Must have current immunizations.

   __ Must pass a physical fitness test.

__ Must be legally able to possess firearms in the state (e.g., no disqualifying convictions).

__ Must meet any state requirements or permits for their individual firearms.

__ Must provide evidence of formal firearms safety training (e.g., police training, military training, NRA training, etc.).

__ Must be willing to provide his or her own equipment (see Minimum Equipment List).

__ Must fill out a written application to volunteer for the security force.

__ Must take the following oath upon acceptance as a volunteer for the security force:[36]

> "I, _____, do solemnly swear (or affirm) that I will support and defend the Constitution of the United States, and the Constitution of the State of ____ against all enemies, foreign and domestic; that I will bear true faith and allegiance to the same; that I will obey the orders of the President of the United States and the orders of the officers appointed over me; that I take this obligation freely,

---

36 To fashion an appropriate oath for the security force, look to the U.S. Armed Forces oath as well as the oath taken by police officers in your state. This sample is a combination.

without any mental reservations or purpose of evasion; and that I will well and faithfully discharge the duties of the militia of the Town of ____, acting to the best of my ability."

MILITIA CODE OF CONDUCT AND GENERAL ORDERS

The U.S. armed forces and every police organization in the country have a code of conduct. Similarly, this is a critical requirement for the militia. A code of conduct and general orders provides the militia with a moral compass. All members of the militia must memorize the code of conduct and general orders, both of which should be recited at militia meetings and trainings. Violations of the code of conduct and general orders are grounds for discipline, up to and including dismissal from service. In time of emergency, the penalties may be more severe.[37]

The code of conduct should be part of the recruiting process and application. Applicants who are selected must agree to abide by the code of conduct. Every member of the militia must carry a copy of the code of conduct on their person at all times.[38]

Code of Conduct

1. I am the guardian of the people of [Town Y] and our way of life. I am prepared to give my life in their defense.
2. I am prepared to suffer and endure hardship, so the town may sleep safely.
3. I will treat all townspeople with respect in all interactions.
4. I will aid and protect those in need to the best of my ability.

---

37 Just as an interesting legal note, the Fifth Amendment to the Constitution provides: "No person shall be held to answer for a capital, or otherwise infamous crime, unless on a presentment or indictment of a Grand Jury, *except in cases arising in the land or naval forces, or in the Militia, when in actual service in time of War or public danger*; nor shall any person be subject for the same offence to be twice put in jeopardy of life or limb; nor shall be compelled in any criminal case to be a witness against himself, nor be deprived of life, liberty, or property, without due process of law; nor shall private property be taken for public use, without just compensation." (emphasis added)

38 Issuing laminated wallet cards at the time of selection is a good way to meet this requirement.

5. I will never lie or engage in any conduct that would bring discredit to my unit or the town.

6. I will serve the people and the town of [Town Y] with honor and integrity.

General Orders (modified slightly from U.S. Army)

1. I will guard everything within the limits of my post and quit my post only when properly relieved.

2. I will obey my special orders and perform all my duties in a professional manner.

3. I will report violations of my special orders, emergencies, and anything not covered in my instructions to the commander.

MINIMUM INDIVIDUAL EQUIPMENT LIST
Uniform[39]

__ Two sets of uniform (BDU)[40] cargo pants, OD green [41]
__ Two sets of uniform (BDU) shirts, OD green
    __ [Town Y] Civil Defense unit patch on the left shoulder
    __ American flag (full color, reversed) on the right shoulder

---

39 There are several good reasons for the militia to be uniformed. First, it presents a professional appearance to the townspeople—and conveys an air of authority to those who come in contact with it. The presence of a uniformed security force will discourage crime and contribute to a feeling of security for the townspeople. Second, uniform standards promote discipline and esprit de corps in the unit. Finally, it makes the militia easily identifiable to citizens who may need assistance. There will likely be no shortage of people running around in hunting garb, carrying guns. The citizens need to be able to easily identify "the good guys" for their safety.

40 Acronym for "Battle Dress Uniform" which was the army's standard combat uniform for many years.

41 "OD" is olive drab green. There are many options, but I'm suggesting OD green uniforms since they are less common than other uniform patterns, such as woodland or ACU pattern camouflage. This will aid the citizens and the units in "friendly force" identification. They would also be easier to maintain and produce than a camouflage pattern.

__ Name tape over the right breast pocket, OD green, black letters

__ "[Town Y] Civil Defense" name tape over the left breast pocket, OD green, black letters

__ Four T-shirts, OD green

__ BDU belt (OD green or black)

__ One uniform "boonie" hat, OD green (warm-weather headgear)

__ One black watch cap (cold-weather headgear)

__ Warm-weather military or hiking boots (tactical color, i.e., black, brown, tan, OD)

__ Cold-weather insulated military or hiking boots (tactical color)

__ 4 pairs of wool socks

__ 1 field jacket (M-65), OD green (with same name tapes and patches as shirts)

__ 1 field jacket liner (M-65), OD green

__ Gloves, OD green or black

__ Thermal underwear (e.g., polypro or similar)

__ Optional but recommended: wool scarf (OD green or black)

__ Optional but recommended: balaclava headgear (OD green or black)

Weapons (note: weapons must comply with state laws and be legally owned and possessed):

__ Rifle or Shotgun with sling

    __ Rifle:[42]

        __ Carried: 200 rounds ammo carried in magazines or stripper clips

        __ Ammo pouches to accommodate the above

---

42 It is recommended that weapons be chambered for commonly available ammunition, such as .22LR, 5.56mm, 7.62x39mm, 7.62x51mm NATO and so on. The only ammo that will be available is what individuals or the group have stored. Exotic ammo will be a problem to obtain or cross level if ammo runs short.

__ Shotgun:
    __ Carried: 100 rounds ammo, 50 percent slugs, 50 percent 00 buckshot
    __ Ammo pouches to accommodate the above
__ Optional: Handgun with extra magazines (*only* if carrier has a pistol permit)
__ Recommended dry storage: At least 2,000 rounds of ammo for primary weapon. At least 500 rounds for each sidearm.

Individual Field Equipment

__ Small field pack, tactical color (small or medium ALICE pack[43] will do)
__ Load Bearing Equipment (LBE) or Load Bearing Vest (LBV)
__ Cleaning kit for weapon(s)
__ 2 canteens or water bottles (1 qt. minimum each) with covers
__ Water purification tablets (watch the expiration dates)
__ Individual first aid kit
__ Poncho or rain suit (OD green, camouflage, or black)
__ Rubber boots (tactical color)
__ Sleeping bag with waterproof "bivy bag" cover (or poncho liner and poncho)
__ Ammo pouches
__ 50 feet of paracord ("550 cord")
__ Compass
__ Topographic and street maps of town (in Ziploc® bag)
__ Protractor (proper scale for topographic map)
__ Small notebook and pen (in Ziploc® bag)

---

43 ALICE is another cryptic acronym: All-purpose Lightweight Individual Carrying Equipment. Don't think for a moment that the army could simply say "backpack."

__ Flashlight with red lens filter (and extra batteries)
__ Knife (KA-BAR® type is fine)
__ Multitool (e.g., Gerber®, Leatherman®, etc.)
__ Small toiletries kit with personal hygiene items
__ Long shelf life rations (3-day supply)
__ Folding shovel
__ Lighter, waterproof matches, and magnesium fire starter
__ For medics: M3 or M5 medic bag (or similar)
__ Optional: knee pads (tactical color)
__ Optional: gaiters (tactical color, i.e., OD green or black)
__ Optional: any other cold weather "snivel gear" you are willing to carry
__ Optional: binoculars
__ Optional: small field stove and metal canteen cup
__ Optional: tent stakes and additional poncho/tarp (tactical color)

UNIT EQUIPMENT

It is equally important to think of equipment that the security force as a whole will need in order to operate in the long term. These are items that individuals probably can't provide themselves. Here are a few ideas:

__ Communications equipment/radios (stored in Faraday cages)
__ Night vision devices (stored in Faraday cages)
__ Handheld GPS devices (stored in Faraday cages)[44]
__ Solar battery chargers/generators (stored in Faraday cages)
__ Extra rechargeable batteries for all equipment (stored in Faraday cages)
__ Binoculars
__ Topographic maps, road maps, compasses, protractors

---

44 I have read that GPS satellites may be affected by an EMP—or by loss of control by the ground equipment—but as nobody knows for sure, I suppose it's worth a shot.

__ Equipment needed for roadblocks and barricades
   __ HESCO Barriers
   __ Concertina wire
   __ Sawhorse barriers
__ Large signs:
   __ "Do Not Enter—Town Residents Only—Armed Patrols on Duty"
   __ "Access Prohibited—Armed Patrols on Duty"
__ Overhead canopies for static posts
__ Long shelf life field rations
__ Portable water purification equipment and filters
__ Ammunition in common calibers used by militia
__ Medic bags (M3 and M5) and medical supplies
__ Extra uniforms, boots, patches[45]
__ Extra individual field equipment[46]
__ Weapons cleaning equipment
__ Field litters/stretchers
__ Tents
__ 5-gallon water cans
__ Ballistic vests/plates/headgear
__ Gas masks, carriers, and extra filters
__ Consider riot control gear
__ Consider EMP-hardened vehicles

Structure of the Security Force

There is no need to reinvent the wheel here. The security force should be structured as a military/paramilitary unit, which also happens to fit ICS span of control principles.[47] Here is a typical structure (based on a combat support military police unit):

---

45 For replacement and issue to new members after an event.

46 For replacement and issue to new members after an event.

47 Incident Command System (ICS) is a system used by emergency management organizations.

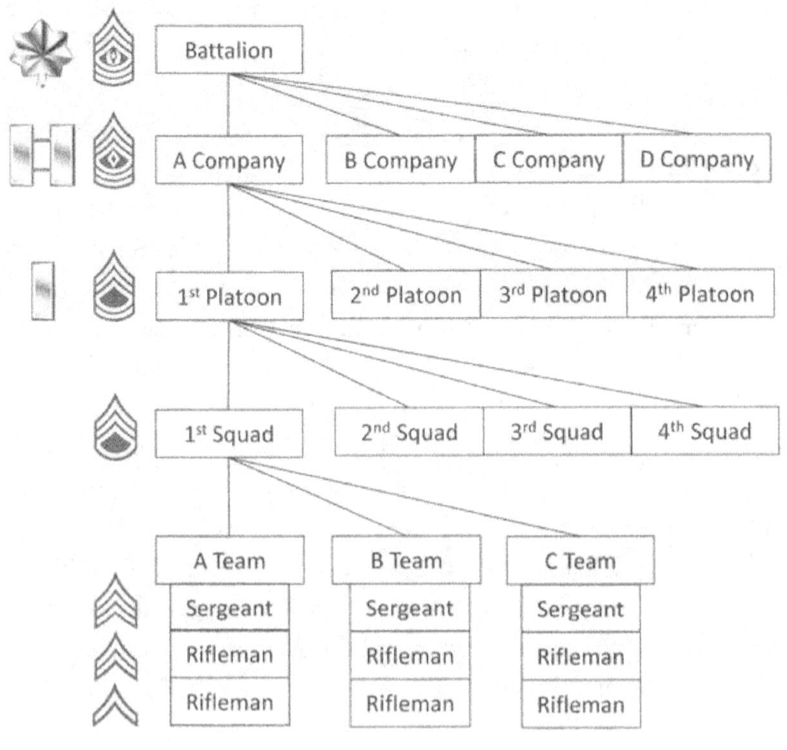

Team:	3 soldiers, led by a team leader (sergeant)
Squad:	3 teams, led by a squad leader (staff sergeant);
Platoon:	3–4 squads, led by a platoon leader (lieutenant), who is assisted by a platoon sergeant (sergeant first class); often includes an RTO (radio operator) and medic
Company:	3–4 platoons, led by a company commander (captain), who is assisted by a first sergeant
Battalion:	3–4 companies, led by a battalion commander (lt. colonel), who is assisted by a command sergeant major

In the army, a full-up company would be an organization of about 120–190 soldiers, and a full-up battalion would be an organization of about 300–1,000 soldiers. A company- or battalion-sized militia is probably a sufficient organizational level for most towns. Before an event, the squads and platoons will likely be smaller (i.e., squads may have two teams, platoons may have three squads, companies may have three platoons, and a battalion organization may be in the low hundreds).

The size of the militia unit in a town will depend on several factors, including the size and population of the town and the geographical features of the town. If there are only one or two roads into and out of a rural town, with natural barriers (rivers, lakes, and mountains) that limit access, the town can get away with a smaller-sized unit. For a suburban town with a lot of roads crossing the borders, you would need a more substantial sized unit.

There is a clear chain of command in this structure, and it also lends itself to decentralized operations, which may be critical in an environment of limited communications and transportation. For example, in a battalion-sized militia unit, the battalion commander reports to the police chief. Each company commander (who reports to the battalion commander) would be in charge of a geographical area of town, and the platoons and squads would be assigned to specific areas, tasks, and operations. They can conduct 24-hour operations by rotating the squads and platoons as needed.

This structure has worked for the U.S. military since 1775, so I don't see a need to try and invent something better. The "peacetime" organization may be a skeleton crew or cadre; in a long-term catastrophe, others in the town would be recruited and trained based on the needs of the town, and many of the existing cadre would likely assume leadership roles. The most important thing is having a structure of trained professionals and plans in place; it would be hard to create this from scratch once the lights go out.

As a practical matter, it would be ideal for a town militia (especially in towns with a lot of square miles to cover) to set up the subordinate units geographically. Volunteers who live in the north part of town would be Company A, volunteers in the south part of town would be Company B, and so on. This way, in a "transportation challenged environment" (due to EMP damage or lack of fuel), the militia can operate largely on foot to cover their "AOs" (areas of operations). The term *area of operations* means the area for which a particular unit is responsible. In other words, the commander of Company B is responsible for security, checkpoints, refugee operations, and so on, in his or her AO. (For smaller towns, substitute "platoon" for "company" in the example above.)

Areas of operations of subordinate units should be clearly defined, using easily identifiable geographic boundaries, such as roads, streams, lakes, and so on. Every inch of the town should fall within the AO of one of the units. If there is a current police department, and they have the town divided into districts, this may be a good start.

The organization needs to do as much planning as possible ahead of time and should develop standing orders and plans for various scenarios, such as control of border crossings, refugee operations, neighborhood patrols, security of town assets, and so on. Don't depend on computer files—all plans and standing orders should be kept in hard copy and be available to the chain of command.

If, after an EMP, a company commander is stuck outside of the town for a week, somebody in the chain of command must be ready to pick up the ball on day one. For each leader in the organization, ask: "If Captain Jones is not here the day the balloon goes up, who steps in?" Make sure that the chain of command is understood by everyone from the top down to the bottom of the structure.

Leadership Qualifications

Once your civil defense organization has decided on a structure for the militia, you will need to fill the key leadership positions. OK, I understand that Joshua Chamberlain was a college professor with no military experience before he became the commander of the 20th Maine, saved the Union's hide at Gettysburg, and was awarded the Medal of Honor. That wasn't typical. While there are some rare "born leaders" out there, the vast majority of us needed to be trained.

Leadership appointments must be made on merit and leadership experience, not because somebody "is a great guy/gal." One place to look is actual military leadership experience. There may be a retired colonel in town who has actually been a battalion or brigade commander and has a proven track record. There may be others in town with military leadership training and experience at various levels. There may be people with law enforcement or civilian leadership experience who can be considered.

After the initial appointments are made for leadership positions in the civil defense security force, a "promotion board" system should be devised to promote from within for future vacancies. As the organization grows and becomes more mature, there should be a clear procedure on how promotions will work. In the future, leadership potential will also be able to be assessed from performance within the security force in training exercises and civil defense activities, as well as past résumé. So, initially, look for:

- Military leadership schools
- Military leadership experience
- Law enforcement leadership schools
- Law enforcement leadership experience
- Civilian leadership training
- Civilian leadership experience

And always look for evidence showing the candidate demonstrates:

- Loyalty, duty, respect, selfless service, honor, integrity, and personal courage[48]

Later, we can add:

- Leadership and performance in the civil defense organization

In army noncommissioned officer (NCO) promotions, soldiers first have to meet the basic requirements (time in grade, time in service, completion of

---

48 From "Army Values," http://www.army.mil/values/index.html (accessed August 28, 2017).

certain training and requirements, etc.), and then they have to attend a promotion board, which is a combination of an interview and a test. The promotion system in the militia should be similar. The basic requirements, necessarily, will likely be more résumé-based, such as past leadership training and experience. There is a free study guide for army promotion boards available at:

http://www.armystudyguide.com.

Although not everything will be applicable, there are a lot of great basic questions (and the answers and references) that can be used on promotion boards for a militia. For example, we would want the future leaders in the militia to know:

- What are the two most important responsibilities of a leader?[49]
- What is the number one principle of peacetime training?[50]
- What are the four fundamentals of marksmanship?[51]
- What are contour lines (on a topographic map)?[52]
- What must be done to a map before it can be used?[53]
- What soldiers are most likely to suffer heat injuries?[54]
- What are the lifesaving steps (the ABCs of medical treatment)?[55]

Then you would want to add some items specific to your organization, mission, and area, such as:

- Recite the [Town Y] militia's code of conduct
- Recite the [Town Y] militia's general orders

---

49 Mission accomplishment and the welfare of the soldiers.

50 Replicate battlefield conditions.

51 (1) Steady Position, (2) Proper Aim (Sight Picture), (3) Breathing, (4) Trigger Squeeze.

52 Imaginary lines on the ground connecting equal elevation, they represent high and low ground elevation.

53 It must be oriented.

54 Soldiers not accustomed to the heat; overweight soldiers; prior heat casualties; and soldiers already dehydrated due to alcohol use, diarrhea, or lack of water.

55 (1) Open the airway and restore breathing, (2) stop the bleeding/protect the wound, (3) prevent shock.

- Find on the topographic map the location of
    - The town hall
    - The police station
    - The hospital (or where it would be established)
    - Emergency muster points

Training

There is no need to reinvent the wheel here, either. The tasks that the militia needs to be trained on are primarily the same tasks that an army military police unit would train on, so look to existing and publicly available training publications from the U.S. Army. You should obtain several hardcopies of each. (Don't depend on computers—you will still need to train people after the grid goes down!)

The other issue to consider is time. You will never have enough time for training. Even if you had a highly motivated group that was willing to each volunteer one day a month, that is only 12 training days a year. Training is the militia leadership's number one priority.[56]

To break several doctrinal manuals down into a few paragraphs (training gods, forgive me), the commander develops a "Mission Essential Task List" (METL) for the unit. The METL includes the large, collective tasks that the organization has to perform as a whole to accomplish its mission. Here are examples of possible METL tasks for the militia:

1. Conduct border security operations
2. Conduct refugee operations
3. Conduct area security operations
4. Conduct law and order operations

Each of these METL tasks are complex operations that consist of several different subtasks, known as collective tasks and battle drills. In order to do the

---

56 U.S. Army FM 7-0. *Train to Win in a Complex World*, p. 1-1.

METL task, the units have to perform these various collective tasks and battle drills.[57] The collective tasks and drills are further broken down into individual tasks. In order for the units to do the collective tasks and drills, each individual soldier has to be able to perform the individual tasks.

For example, in order to perform the METL task of "Conduct Area Security Operations," a platoon or squad must be able to perform several collective tasks and drills, including "React to Ambush."[58] In order for the squad to do this drill, each individual solder must be able to perform several individual tasks, including "Move Under Direct Fire."[59]

Once the civil defense organization has defined the possible missions for the militia, the militia should develop its own METL, create its own Mission Training Plan (MTP) and battle drills, and extract the individual tasks necessary for to support the drills and collective tasks in the MTP.

With an extremely limited amount of training time, it is critical that the training plan be well crafted and focus on critical individual tasks and small unit (squad level) drills. Developing a "Militia Task Book"—a cargo-pocket-sized book of critical tasks, drills, and checklists that the militia members can carry—is a great idea.

Here are some of the U.S. Army references from which you can extract many of the individual tasks you will need[60]:

Individual Tasks:
STP 21-1-SMCT (Soldiers Manual of Common Tasks Skill Level 1)
STP 21-24-SMCT (Soldiers Manual of Common Tasks Skill Level 2–4)

---

57 "A battle drill is a collective action executed by a platoon or smaller element without the application of a deliberate decision making process. The action is vital to success in combat or critical to preserve life. The drill is initiated on a cue, such as an enemy action or simply a leader's order, and is a trained response to the given stimulus. It requires minimum leader orders to accomplish and is standard throughout the Army." U.S. Army ARTEP 19-100-10-DRILL, p. 1-1

58 See U.S. Army ARTEP 7-8-DRILL, Battle Drill 07-3-D9105—React to Ambush (Platoon/Squad).

59 See U.S. Army STP 21-1-SMCT, Task # 071-326-0502, Move Under Direct Fire.

60 Many valuable U.S. Army publications are available from the Army Publishing Directorate website at http://www.apd.army.mil/ (accessed August 28, 2017).

STP 19-31B1-SM (Soldiers Manual MP Skill Level 1)
STP 19-31B24-SM-TG (Soldier's Manual and Trainer's Guide MP, Skill Levels 2–4)
STP 7-11B1-SM-TG (Soldier's Manual and Trainer's Guide, Infantry, Skill Level 1)
STP 7-11B24-SM-TG (Soldier's Manual and Trainer's Guide, Infantry, Skills Level 2–4)

Here are some examples of drills and MTPs. You will be able to glean some applicable drills and collective tasks from these and see examples of how to set them up.

Battle drills:
 ARTEP 19-100-10-DRILL (Military Police Drills)
 ARTEP 7-8-Drill (Battle Drills for the Infantry Rifle Platoon and Squad)

Collective tasks:
 ARTEP 19-313-10-MTP (Mission Training Plan EOC MP Platoon)
 ARTEP 19-313-30-MTP (Mission Training Plan EOC MP Company)
 ARTEP 7-8-MTP (Mission Training Plan for the Infantry Rifle Platoon and Squad)
 ARTEP 7-10-MTP (Mission Training Plan for the Infantry Rifle Company)

Further doctrinal guidance may be found in:
 FM 2-19.4 (Military Police Leaders' Handbook)
 FM 3-21.8 (The Infantry Rifle Platoon and Squad)

It would seem that the four sample METL tasks for the militia above cover many of the anticipated challenges facing a town in a long-term national catastrophe where the town finds itself without outside help, including:

- Security of assets and neighborhoods
  - Security of businesses/neighborhoods from looters and crime

> o   Security of water, food sources, and critical infrastructure
> o   Securing entryways into the community
- Management of refugees
> o   Securing entryways into the community
> o   Escort through (and out) of the community
> o   Establishing and controlling refugee camps (if practical)

Missions of the Militia

The militia's orders and missions will come from the civilian leadership of the town. For example, the town may wish to provide aid to refugees to the extent that resources allow. Some thought should be given to locations and necessary resources for refugee camps or food and water distribution points, if this becomes a mission for the militia. On the other hand, if the decision is made by the town that resources are not available to assist the refugees, then the militia's mission could be to escort them safely through and out of town and to secure the town borders.

Many of the likely missions can, for the most part, be anticipated. Detailed reconnaissance, plans, and training should be completed ahead of time. Using the examples above of the METL tasks, here are some considerations. Every town militia will have a slightly different mission set due to geography and resources, but this discussion can provide a starting point.

MISSION: CONDUCT BORDER SECURITY OPERATIONS

There are 26 roads that cross the border of Town Y. The majority are local residential roads. There are four numbered state roads, which would be the most likely to be used by refugees. Of these, two lead directly to urban areas and would be the most likely main routes of refugee traffic. There are also four additional town roads, which are main roads leading to and from neighboring towns. In a few instances, more than one minor road could be covered by a single team, because they are close enough together.[61]

---

61 This is an incredibly resource-intensive mission. In this example, if you wanted to cover 26 roads 24/7 with at least a three-person team, working 12-hour shifts, you would need 156 people

At each road crossing, the border needs to be studied in detail to determine the likelihood of refugee traffic and the type of security needed. Both map reconnaissance and actual physical reconnaissance are needed for each crossing. Topographic maps are necessary to see what the geography of the area is, beyond what you can see on the ground. Also, topographic maps may reveal other areas of concern besides roads, such as trails or areas that are easily crossed by foot. A security plan for every potential crossing area into town needs to be formulated and placed in the border security plan for each unit's area of responsibility. Perhaps, if manpower is limited, the commander would decide that some remote roads would not be manned 24 hours a day. They may instead be covered by barriers and signs ("Do Not Enter—Town Residents Only—Armed Patrols on Duty") and occasional patrols. Other more likely routes would be covered by 24-hour manned access control points.

This example presents a typical analysis. On the topographic map below,[62] the road crosses the town border at Point A. However, a little farther southwest is a trail (the dashed line intersecting the road at Point B) that leads over a dam and crosses into Town Y on the other side of the reservoir. Due to the steep elevation in the terrain, it appears unlikely that Point B would be visible from Point A. It also appears unlikely that the dam or the trail would be visible from Point A. This was confirmed by physical reconnaissance. So, in order to cover both the road and the trail into Town Y, it would be necessary to place the access control point at Point B. In fact, there is a bridge just to the southwest of Point B, which allows excellent visibility for a good distance and makes this an ideal spot for a militia access control point.

The only other option would be to have access control points both at Point A and at the Town Y border on the east side of the dam. This would require additional manpower and, in looking at the terrain on the ground, it

---

(two shifts of 78 each). This is why assessment and planning ahead of time is critical. You may not have the resources to cover everything with your initial cadre until more people can be recruited and trained after the event. And some major entryways may require several teams or even squads to cover. Commanders will have to implement the best plan they can with available resources.

62 U.S. Geological Survey map.

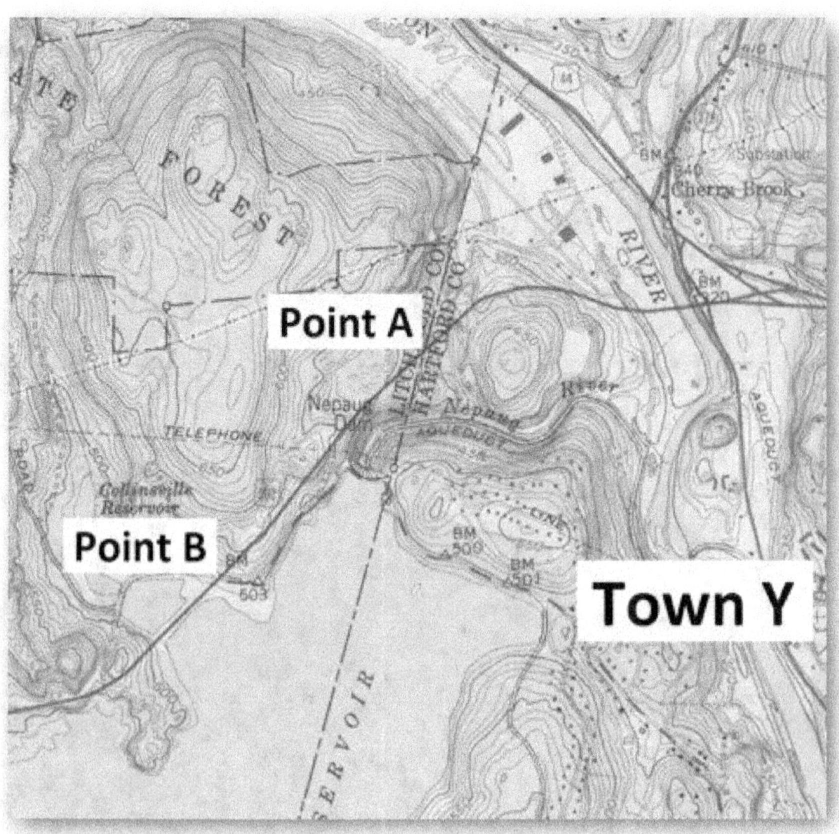

appears that it would be difficult to control people who see the access control point and descend the hill to the dry river bed—which is essentially another trail into Town Y. Point B is, therefore, the best option for an access control point.

A terrain analysis and physical reconnaissance needs to be conducted on every entryway into the town, so that you can begin to formulate plans to control the border crossings. The militia needs to know every road, trail, or likely crossing point on the town's borders and know how they can control access at those points with the most efficient use of their available personnel.

Take advantage of technology while you have it. The below satellite image is from the U.S. Geological Survey. It shows a detail of the area of we just discussed. You'd be surprised at what you find when you sweep the border of your town "by satellite." It would be wise to have a topographic map and a satellite image of every border crossing printed up and included with the plan.

One final thought on the border security mission: if this mission is accomplished well, fewer resources may be required for other missions, such as area security and law enforcement operations.

MISSION: CONDUCT REFUGEE OPERATIONS

Any town that has roads leading to urban areas needs to plan for the management of refugees. Geography and proximity to urban areas will affect how many refugees and how soon after a catastrophe. The only thing we can predict with certainty is that without power, food, services, and transportation, urban areas will quickly lose their ability to support their large human populations. At some point, people are going to begin to flee.

The town's decisions on the handling of refugees will obviously be different in a local or regional disaster, where outside resources are available or anticipated. In that case, the town is likely to do whatever it can to assist the refugees with food, shelter, and medical attention until state or federal aid arrives—and the civil defense organization will be prepared to assist.

A long-term national catastrophe, in which no outside resources are available or anticipated, presents other challenges for town leaders. What if there is not enough food and other resources for the town itself? Will the town be able to assist hundreds, thousands or tens of thousands of additional people arriving from the urban areas? The militia must be prepared and trained to handle two general scenarios:

1. If the town decides that it *can* provide assistance to refugees: The militia executes the plan for establishing and protecting humanitarian assistance areas, where the refugees would receive whatever shelter, food, and medical support that the town is able to provide.
2. If the town decides that it *cannot* provide assistance to refugees: The militia executes the plan for management of refugees by routing them around or escorting them through and out of the town.

Detailed plans for both scenarios need to be drawn up ahead of time, so the militia can quickly respond to their orders. Training plans should cover both possibilities and joint training with other parts of the civil defense organization (e.g., the medical section) should be conducted.

"Refugees and IDPs [Internally Displaced Persons] present a complex scenario for the military. What makes this more challenging is the limited military doctrine on refugee and IDP operations."[63] However, the army recently

---

63 United States Army Combined Arms Center, Center for Army Lessons Learned, *Commander's Guide to Supporting Refugees and Internally Displaced Persons,* issue 12-21. Fort Leavenworth, KS. September 2012. Page 100. http://cgsc.contentdm.oclc.org/cdm/ref/collection/p15040coll4/id/42 (accessed August 2, 2017) or http://usacac.army.mil/sites/default/files/publications/12-21.pdf (accessed August 2, 2017).

published a handbook called *Commander's Guide to Supporting Refugees and Internally Displaced Persons*; it contains a great deal of information that will be helpful, particularly Chapter 9, "Health and Sanitation for Displaced Persons;" Chapter 10, "The Challenges of Liquid Logistics in Refugee and Internally Displaced Persons Camps;" Chapter 12, "Security Considerations for Military Commanders Establishing or Protecting a Refugee Camp;" and Chapter 13, "Key Military Police Tasks in Refugee/Internally Displaced Persons Operations: Providing Security and Preventing Human Suffering." The civil defense organization should study this document while devising its plans. It is available at:

http://usacac.army.mil/sites/default/files/publications/12-21.pdf (as a PDF file).

If refugee escort through (and out of) town is anticipated on a border crossing, additional resources and plans will be needed to accomplish this escort. This will most likely be in Town Y's case, on the two main roads leading to and from the urban areas.

Finally, it is essential to remember who the refugees are: Americans. Commanders must be vigilant to ensure that their teams are treating refugees with respect and offering whatever assistance the town has authorized.

MISSION: CONDUCT AREA SECURITY OPERATIONS

As there will likely be too few people in the security force (militia) to have somebody stationed on every corner, and transportation will likely be a challenge (i.e., most operations will be conducted on foot), the militia can conduct area security operations similar to military police, which will allow them to cover larger areas with smaller units. The militia may adopt some of the techniques discussed in FM 2-19.4 Military Police Leaders' Handbook, Chapter 6, as well as FM 3-21.8 The Infantry Rifle Platoon and Squad, Chapters 3 and 9.

The commander will identify critical areas, such as:

- Water sources
- Food sources and farms

- Supply warehouses
- High-value assets
- Likely infiltration routes into town
- At-risk neighborhoods (such as near borders, or isolated areas)

The platoon leaders and squad leaders will plan and conduct area security patrols using standard troop leading procedures (TLPs)[64] and pre-combat inspections (PCIs).[65]

MISSION: CONDUCT LAW AND ORDER OPERATIONS
The militia may be given the mission to Conduct Law and Order Operations. This could occur immediately after the blackout (e.g., protect business areas and critical assets from looters and criminals) as well as on a long-term basis in a national catastrophe where traditional police assets are overtaxed or unavailable.

Immediate Actions after an Event
It would be advisable that the militia have specific standing orders when a "blackout" is identified as not routine. For example, in a blackout where electronics appear to be affected, such as battery-operated electronic devices, radios, and communications devices, and there are other indications of an EMP or large-scale event, the members of the militia should know exactly where to report and with what equipment, so they may be immediately deployed.

Longer-term Actions
Where there are some police assets available, such as a small number of police officers, the militia would supplement and take direction from this force in accordance with orders of the police chief. Where there is no police

---

64 FM 2-19.4 Military Police Leaders' Handbook, Chapter 2; FM 3-21.8 The Infantry Rifle Platoon and Squad, Chapter 5.

65 FM 2-19.4 Military Police Leaders' Handbook, Appendix E.

department, the militia commander should be prepared to assume the law and order operations mission upon order of the town government.

In the absence of a police department, two army references will be helpful in training for and conducting the law and order operations mission: ATTP 3-39-10 Law and Order Operations and FM 3-19.13 Law Enforcement Investigations.

Six

OTHER CONSIDERATIONS OF THE CIVIL DEFENSE PLAN

Long-term sustainable solutions are the best goals in a long-term catastrophe, when it is unclear when—or if—the grid and supply chain may be restored. But because some of these may take significant time, interim measures to "bridge the gap" need to be in the civil defense organization's plan.

For example, there may be a long-term plan for sustainable food production, but it is unknown in what season the power may go out and it will take a substantial amount of time to get food production up and running. The town may have to survive for many months on what it has in the cupboard. An interim plan should focus on several areas: First, education and outreach to encourage families to increase their own food storage. Second, the organization may want to look into bulk emergency storage. Third, protecting from looters any grocery stores, schools, restaurants, and other places where bulk food may be stored is also critical to preserve the available food supply. Finally, steps should be taken to preserve as much of the existing food supply as possible immediately after an event, such as preserving some perishable foods.

Below are some considerations for the four major sections (Planning, Operations, Logistics and Finance) and their subgroups.

I. Planning Section Considerations

The planning section's core function before an emergency is to compile data and ideas from each of the other sections and teams, as well as forming plans for the organization that can be implemented. The planning section serves as the nerve center, where the work of the various sections and groups is collated and incorporated into plans. The leadership of the organization will rely on the data compiled by the planning section to make resource decisions.

The second interrelated core function is working with the town government to integrate the civil defense organization into the town's emergency planning. This may be in the form of working with the town to identify what the anticipated resources and needs would be in a long-term catastrophe, and how the civil defense organization can work to bridge the gap. It will also be in the form of working with the community (through the finance and community outreach section) to raise awareness of emergency preparedness and to locate resources and skills within the community.

For example: The town government and the civil defense organization realize that, in their area of the country, winters without heat would place the population at risk. The civil defense organization's planning section can send a "task request" to the logistics section, for the alternative power, equipment, and skills team to come up with methods and plans to safely heat homes using materials and construction methods that would be available after an event. The team comes back with plans to build wood-burning stoves from the hot water heaters in the basements of many houses and parts from cars. Although all the raw materials are present in the town to retrofit the majority of houses with wood stoves, other resource needs are identified: welders, welding equipment, and welding gas. The planning section can place these skills and resources on the list of items that the organization will work to acquire. The outreach people may talk to business owners in town who have welding operations (such as automotive businesses) and get an idea of how many welders may be town residents. These business owners and employees may be important people to get involved in the logistics section. When completed, the town will have a plan to enable people to survive the winter cold—and have a cooking method to boot! Instead of being caught flat-footed in modern houses with no electricity, there is now a plan in place to provide a long-term solution.

Some of the products of the planning section would include:

- Detailed contingency plans for security, food, water, and shelter needs of the town in the event of a long-term catastrophe.
- An "activation plan," so that the organization and town can recognize a national catastrophe as quickly as possible and critical functions of the organization can self-activate (e.g., militia reports to police station, schools activate "get home" plan for children, critical civil defense personnel know where to report and what to do).
- Booklets for distribution to townspeople before and after an event, detailing critical information, techniques, and plans they will need to build latrines, wood-burning stoves, water collection and purification systems, trash disposal systems, and so on.
- Finding ways to develop, acquire, and store resources that the various sections identify as critical.
- Planning for training drills.
- Facilitating collaborative efforts between the teams.

You will see many areas of overlap between the various sections. For example, the alternative power, equipment, and skills team may be looking at alternative skills and equipment needed for 1880s-style agriculture. This will be a concern for the food team as well. The militia will be one of the primary users of communications and will need to work with the communications team.

Where interests overlap, the planning section can bring the groups together to collaborate and devise plans that will satisfy the concerns of multiple groups, instead of going at similar problems individually.

II. Operations Section Considerations

The previous Chapter touched on the security force (militia). Below are a few more considerations for the operations section and its major teams.

Medical Team Considerations

Power and critical infrastructure loss will bring us to a third-world level in terms of medicine. The only difference between our town and a village in

Africa is that the villagers in Africa have an advantage—they are used to it, have survived it, and likely have some immunities built up. We will be starting out as a pampered, overweight modern society, suddenly thrust into 1880. Making matters worse, we have to plan for no outside contact and no medical resupply for a substantial period of time—perhaps a year or more.

It is an absolute medical nightmare. Pacemaker patients, dialysis patients, insulin-dependent diabetics, organ transplant patients, patients whose lives depend on medications for a variety of reasons—and suddenly there are no more machines and medications. The medical plan must address what needs to be done to provide at least a minimum level of medical services for the town and mitigate the loss of life wherever possible.

A few initial considerations:

- If the town were isolated and without power for a year or more, what medical facilities, equipment, and supplies would be needed to provide the townspeople with at least a minimum of medical services?
- What medical professionals (doctors, nurses, paramedics, EMTs) would be likely to be in town and available?
- What medical electronic equipment would be most critical and would need to be protected from an EMP/solar flare?
- What critical medications and supplies can be stockpiled and stored for the long term?
- What patients would be immediately at risk, and what steps can be taken to save them?
- What patients would be at risk when medications become scarce, and what steps can be taken to save them?
- What diseases and injuries would we expect in a long-term outage, with the resulting decrease in nutrition and exposure to the environment? What prevention measures could be taken? What would be needed to respond?
- What alternatives to common medications (e.g., antibiotics) might be available and what needs to be done ahead of time to facilitate alternatives?

- Is it prudent to recommend certain immunizations for critical personnel before the grid goes down—especially for the security team (militia) and medical team, who may be exposed to diseases from refugees?
- If transportation is limited, how can medical services best be provided to the town? Would medical teams stationed at firehouses, for example, adequately cover the needs—and are there enough personnel to accomplish this?

COMMUNICATIONS TEAM CONSIDERATIONS

Modern communications equipment is particularly vulnerable to an EMP or solar flare. Even in a "best-case / worst-case" scenario, where the grid goes down but equipment is not damaged, power is needed. When fuel is depleted for backup generators, the communications goes down.

Protection of at least a minimal amount of communications equipment as well as alternative power sources is an important consideration. A few good-quality walkie-talkies and solar battery chargers in a Faraday cage would be a godsend in a crisis. The town in Chapter 2 actually devised a messenger service as a sustainable solution to its communications needs. A long-term plan would likely want to consider a combination of good EMP protection for a stockpile of critical equipment, as well as some low-tech long-term communications solutions.

Internal Communications

The town government, militia and other town services will need internal communications in place quickly after a worst-case event (such as an EMP strike or solar flare). What types of communications equipment should be acquired and protected in Faraday cages? What other types of communications should be developed or considered? Consider:

- Two-way radios
- Wired field phones (e.g., old-school TA-312s and SB-22/PT)
- Batteries and chargers
- Alternate signaling techniques/messenger techniques and systems

External Communications

The town government will also need a means of monitoring and transmitting to outside entities. Here are some ideas:

- HAM/shortwave radios in Faraday cages
- Shortwave receivers in Faraday cages
- Satellite communications devices in Faraday cages

SAFETY, HEALTH, AND SANITATION TEAM CONSIDERATIONS

If the fire department has limited ability to respond, smoke and carbon monoxide detectors are no longer working, and people are without traditional means of heating and cooking, the threat to life from fire increases.

If sewage systems do not work and garbage is not being collected, the threat of disease and contamination of water supplies increases.

And if people who spent their lives working at a desk in an office suddenly have to chop wood, haul water long distances on their backs, and do atypical and hazardous tasks, the risk of injuries and fatalities from accidents will increase.

Health and safety awareness and preparation of training materials on proper techniques to accomplish nontraditional tasks are some of the responsibilities of the safety, health, and sanitation team—*before* an event. After an event, elements of the team may report to the town fire marshal, fire chief, or health department to conduct outreach, training, and intervention to guard the health and safety of the town.

- Plans for how (and where) to build latrines that can be built by average people.
- Plans for how (and where) to dispose of rubbish.
- Fire safety outreach materials; if cold and without heat, people may do unsafe things in their houses to stay warm.
- Plans for building and retrofitting houses with wood-burning stoves and fireplaces from available materials (working with the alternative power, equipment, and skills team).
- What can be done in the winter for families with little or no heat?

- What supplies should be stockpiled and stored?
- What safety measures can be taken to train/protect people attempting to perform unfamiliar work?
- How should neighborhoods respond to a fire in the absence of traditional fire equipment?

Legal Team Considerations

The town may need to establish a court. If there is a group of lawyers in the town, this is a great job for them—they can design a court system to fit the needs of the town. (This will likely require the town to pass a law after the event, establishing the court.) Lawyers are also trained in dispute resolution—and there could be a lot of disputes to resolve. Effectively handling disputes can help keep the peace. And we thought lawyers wouldn't be useful after the apocalypse!

The town may need to establish new laws (e.g., the fictitious town in Chapter 2 passed a law that all old clothes and cloth could not be thrown away but had to be turned over to the town. This apparently addressed a critical need for blankets and clothes).

- If no court exists, what emergency legislation would the town have to pass to establish one?
- How would criminal and civil proceedings work in an austere environment?
- If the town does not have the resources for a "correctional facility," what other options exist in criminal cases? What emergency laws would be needed to implement such options?
- What dispute resolution services can the court offer for the town and townspeople?

III. Logistics Section Considerations

Water, food, and shelter are the basic human needs for survival. The logistics section is focused on long-term sustainable solutions to these problems, as well as interim solutions to bridge the gap between the power going out and the long-term solutions becoming effective.

Realistically, it will take a great deal of time to get food and water production up and running. It will take a great deal of time and resources to retrofit houses with safe heating and cooking capability. Many people will die in the interim without planning and sufficient food storage, water purification methods, and the regaining of lost survival skills. The logistics section is responsible for developing plans and methods to address the basic survival needs of the town.

Water Team Considerations

- Develop home rainwater collection plans.
- Develop home water purification system plans.
- What large-scale water purification systems are possible to meet the needs of the town?
- How can water be distributed in a transportation-challenged environment?
- What supplies, equipment, and chemicals should be stockpiled?
- Can water purification elements be manufactured in town for a long-term catastrophe?
- Identify critical water sources needing protection by the militia.
- What possible sources of contamination to the critical water sources are likely and what can be done to mitigate contamination?

Food Team Considerations

- Identify areas where bulk food may be presently available (grocery stores, restaurants, schools, etc.) and get a list to the planning section to work into the security plan.
- What can be done with perishable/frozen food initially to increase its usability? What can be quickly preserved?

- What farms already exist, and what do they grow? Without power and possibly some modern equipment, how will the farms still operate?
- Is there other land suitable for large-scale farming in an emergency?
- Are there greenhouses suitable for food production?
- Are there alternative methods of food production possible (e.g., aquaponics, a fish farm)?
- What are the best staple foods for farming in this region?
- What domestic animals, if any, are viable options for long-term food sources (taking into consideration that lack of transportation makes feed an issue)?
- Develop instructions and plans for home gardens and aquaponics systems.
- Where would the town get seeds for crops?
- What food needs to be stored to bridge the gap between the power going out and the advent of sufficient internal food production?
- What are the best staple foods for bulk long-term storage?
- What is the plan to issue ration cards in an emergency?
- What does the town *not* have now that it will need to conduct major agricultural and food production activities?
- What food safety issues will come up in a grid-down scenario?
- If the civil defense organization begins to store bulk food, devise a rotation plan so that food can be donated to charity before the expiration date and is replaced.

ALTERNATIVE POWER, EQUIPMENT, AND SKILLS TEAM CONSIDERATIONS

- Plans for alternative heating and cooking methods that can be fabricated from locally available materials (working with safety, health, and sanitation team).
- Plans for alternatives to power tools and equipment.
- What supplies and skills will be needed to preserve food?

- What supplies and skills will be needed for food production, 1880s style?
- What additional "lost skills" will be useful to the town in a long-term catastrophe?
- Can solar and wind energy be harnessed after a grid-down event? What equipment should be acquired and protected?
- Is it feasible to restore some older EMP-resistant vehicles that burn multiple fuels (including diesel and home heating oil, which can be stored for long periods)? For example, vehicles similar to the army's M35 2.5-ton truck.
- If the civil defense organization begins to store bulk fuel (e.g., home heating oil), devise a rotation plan so that fuel can be donated to charity and is replaced before it goes bad.

IV. Finance and Community Outreach Section

The more successful the organization is at raising funds, the more options are available for long-term preparation. This is one core function of the finance and community outreach section. The other core function is raising awareness of the need for family preparedness. In doing this, the outreach function also seeks to make the civil defense organization an accepted part of the town culture. A successful organization will develop a reputation on par with the fire department, ambulance service, and police department—organizations dedicated to preservation of life and safety.

A few of the considerations will be:

- Planning for fundraising events.
- Conducting community outreach to educate the public on emergency preparedness.
- Educating the public on skills that make them—and the entire town—more self-reliant.

- At some point, storage and meeting space will be needed. Having someone familiar with local real estate in the finance section could be a plus.
- Research the availability of any federal or state grants for the civil defense organization's activities.
- Providing documentation to the treasurer and secretary for completion of mandatory nonprofit reports and returns.

Seven

INDIVIDUAL/FAMILY PREPPING STILL MATTERS

This chapter does not address situations where people would likely have to evacuate their homes in a long-term catastrophe (e.g., people who live in a city or next to a nuclear power plant who would be forced to "bug out"). In a suburban or rural area, assuming that there is no immediate hazard to the home forcing a family to evacuate, there are two basic areas that people should think about on the individual/family preparedness front:

1. What supplies and capabilities should they make sure they have at home?
2. How will they get home if they are stuck elsewhere in a national catastrophe?

Stating the obvious, the more people in the community who are prepared for a long-term catastrophe, the better off the community will be if it happens. Even if more people were prepared for a one-week power outage (or even to the FEMA 72-hour standard) the community will still be better off than it is right now. One of the core missions of the civil defense organization is to educate and prepare the townspeople and town government. The organization can have a tremendous impact just by raising awareness and increasing the number of families in town who have at least a minimum preparedness level.

It is likely that, if the civil defense organization is even partially successful, many people in town may at least give some thought to long-term preparedness. Perhaps not everyone will start to build a one-year food supply, but maybe more people will start collecting a few extra cans and think it prudent to have enough for a month, in case of a longer-than-normal power outage. That would still be great progress. If the civil defense organization is at least getting people thinking and taking some small actions, it is a success.

There are a few sample checklists attached here, and there are many others out there in varying levels of detail, but there is no perfect one-size-fits-all checklist. Each family should be encouraged to develop their own. A possible service that the civil defense organization's community outreach section could offer is consultation services for the town's families to help them develop their emergency plans. We will probably be able to think of some things that many people won't—such as, where are you going to go to the bathroom if the bathroom stops working.

In terms of supplies and capabilities at home, some families might have a fireplace or wood-burning stove and therefore have a safe alternative for heating their house and cooking. Some families' homes may be completely dependent on electricity for everything. Some families may have individuals with medical conditions, requiring additional supplies. Availability of water and means of waste disposal may vary greatly in different parts of town.

In terms of getting home after a catastrophe, some people may work in town and could easily walk home, whereas others may work in a neighboring city or may frequently travel long distances. Almost everybody leaves town at some point to go shopping or visit relatives. A "get-home bag" awareness program can help get the word out to people that they should have some minimal supplies in their vehicles and offices, in case they get caught outside of town.

You can't go wrong in preparedness if you think about the basics, whether for home supplies or get-home bags: water, shelter, food, and clothing. There are lots of other nice-to-have items, but any plan or checklist must cover the basics.

Get-home bags should be based on where somebody typically travels. Somebody who works in an office 10 miles away would have different needs than somebody who frequently travels a long distance on business. Weight is a huge issue. If you are putting together a get-home bag anticipating a multi-day hike home (let's say, 120 miles, or about five to six days), this can easily become over 50 pounds of gear when you pack everything you think you might need. If you can't carry a 50-pound pack for 20 miles a day for five to six days (on reduced rations), then you need to lighten it to the bare minimum you need to survive: water, food, shelter, and clothing. You need to test out your get-home bag on a hike of at least a few miles and make sure you can carry it.

If you are lucky enough to be in an area with numerous lakes and streams, maybe you can get away with carrying less water and packing a water purifier or filter. If you're traveling in an area without much water, you will need to carry a lot of water, and that is really heavy. Have topographic and road maps in your bag of the state(s) you anticipate hiking through—the topographic maps show water sources.

If your typical work clothes are not suitable for a hike home, you need to make sure that you have a good set of boots, socks, and a set of hiking clothes in your car, office, or suitcase. You will also want to make seasonal adjustments to your get-home bag(s). What you need to survive in the winter will likely be different than what you need in the summer, especially with regard to shelter and clothing.

People who frequently travel long distances by air have to split their "get-home bag" between their carry-on luggage and checked luggage—you can't have your KA-BAR° knife in your carry-on luggage. You can reassemble your get-home bag when you get to your destination. If you are one of those annoying people who don't check any bags and just use a huge carry-on, you will have some critical items that you just can't take with you.

Another thing to ponder: If there was an EMP strike, would the hotel room door still open with the key card? I have no idea, but it has been years since I had a hotel room with an actual key. Consider staying on ground-level rooms if you can and carry a small pry bar when you are away from your room. (You can find a small 8-inch pry bar at a hardware store for under $10.) Your get-home bag won't help if you can't get to it. If you rent a car at your destination, you may want to consider keeping your get-home bag in the trunk of the car, rather than in the hotel room.

Finally, the checklists below do not generally address weapons. The choice of weapons (or no weapons) is for an individual to make. A person without a weapon who is able to avoid contact with others and move by stealth may stand a better chance that a well-armed person walking down the center of a main road. There is no right or wrong answer to the weapons question—only what is right for the individual.

That being said, remember that we are not preparing for the world we live in—we are preparing for the world we find ourselves in.

Sample Home Prep Checklist
Short Term (one month or less)

Item	On Hand	Need
Food and water (long shelf life, one month)		
Water purification system w/filters		
Generator (hardwired to house)		
Fuel (one week) w/stabilizer, rotate yearly		
Medical supplies/medications		
Radio AM/FM/NOAA/SW (alt power)*		
Sanitary supplies		
Pet food (one month)		
Solar lights (from yard)		
Solar battery charger/batteries*		
Flashlights		
Duct tape/plastic sheeting		

<u>Assumptions</u>:

- We can stay in the house.
- Gasoline is available.
- Other utilities (water, natural gas, sewer) and essential services are available.

Long-Term (more than one month—in addition to above items)

Item	On Hand	Need
Food (long shelf life, one year)		
Safe alternative cooking methods		
Safe alternative home heating methods		
Sleeping bags rated for area's winter temps		
Faraday cage (*items stored here)		
Alt energy: solar generator/wind turbine*		
Two-way radios (rechargeable)*		
Water (55-gal drums/pump/wrench)		
Water preserver (for 55-gal drums)		
Extra filters for water purification system		
Water cans (5-gal) w/pack to carry		
Lighters/matches		
Medical supplies/medications		
SAS Survival Handbook/books on edible plants		
Sanitary supplies (one year)		
Alternative waste disposal		
Pet food (long shelf life)		
Weapons/ammunition		

Assumptions:

- We can stay in the house.
- Gasoline may not be available.
- Other utilities (water, natural gas, sewer) and essential services may not be available.

Sample Get-Home Bag (Long Distance—Multiple Days)

	Item	On Hand	Need
Water	Backpack (w/frame)		
	Water purification tablets		
	Portable water purifier		
	Coffee filters (for water)		
	Water (emergency packaged)		
	Canteens or stainless steel bottles (2)		
Food	Food/emergency rations		
	Eating utensils		
	Canteen cup/stove/fuel		
	Lighters/matches/magnesium fire starter		
Shelter	Emergency blankets		
	Bivy sack		
	Sleeping bag		
	Paracord, 50 feet		
	Tent stakes		
	Poncho		
Clothes	Watch cap/gloves		
	Boots/socks		
	Cold-weather gear		
	Suitable hiking clothes		
	First aid kit		
	Hand sanitizer		
	Hygiene supplies		
	Folding shovel		
	LED lights/batteries		
	Compass/maps (in Ziploc® bag)		
	Multitool		
	Pocket chainsaw		
	Knife		
	Binoculars		
	Etón Scorpion radio (in Faraday bag)		
	Magnifying glass		
	Estwing® E24A sportsman axe		
	SAS Survival Guide (in Ziploc® bag)		
	Duct tape		
	Small tent		

Note: This bag is really heavy. If you can't realistically carry it, get rid of the tent and folding shovel, and start eliminating items until you can carry the bag. A bag you can't carry will be useless as a get-home bag.

Sample Get-Home Bag (Short Distance—Possibly Overnight)

	Item	On Hand	Need
	Small tactical bag		
Water	Water purification tablets		
	Portable water purifier		
	Coffee filters (for water)		
	Water (emergency packaged)		
	Canteen or stainless steel bottles		
Food	Food/emergency rations		
	Eating utensils		
	Canteen cup/stove/fuel		
	Lighters/matches/magnesium fire starter		
Shelter	Emergency blankets		
	Sleeping bag liner		
	Tent stakes		
	Paracord, 50 feet		
	Poncho		
Clothes	Watch cap/gloves		
	Boots/socks		
	Suitable hiking clothes		
	Cold weather gear		
	Hand sanitizer		
	Hygiene supplies		
	LED lights		
	Compass/maps (in Ziploc® bag)		
	Multitool		
	First aid kit		
	SAS Survival Guide (in Ziploc® bag)		
	Knife		

Sample Get-Home Bag (Cross Country—Air Travel)

	Item	On Hand	Need
Carry-On Bag	Small tactical bag (carry on)		
	Portable water purifier		
	Bivy sack		
	Paracord, 50 feet		
	Emergency blanket		
	Rain gear (poncho)		
	Compass		
	US atlas/maps (in Ziploc® bag)		
	Magnifying glass		
	LED lights		
	AAA batteries		
	Binoculars		
	Book on edible plants (in Ziploc® bag)		
	SAS Survival Handbook (in Ziploc® bag)		
	Coffee filters (for water)		
	Duct tape		
Checked Bag	Military canteen/cup/stove/cover		
	Food/emergency rations		
	Etón Scorpion radio (in Faraday bag)		
	Small sleeping bag (e.g., Eureka!® Hoback)		
	Water purification tabs		
	Boots/socks		
	Suitable hiking clothes		
	Small first aid kit		
	Eating utensils		
	Lighters/matches/mag fire starter		
	Small pry bar (carry at destination)		
	Tent stakes		
	Multitool		
	Emergency saw		
	Knife		
	Estwing® E24A sportsman axe		

Travel bag (small tactical bag/carry on)
Travel Kit (checked)

Note: You can play with what you carry on versus what is in your checked baggage. Check with TSA's website to see what may be a problem for the carry-on. You can save space by wearing your boots and a set of clothes suitable for hiking.

Eight

Aquaponics—A Food Solution

Producing food is critical to a community's survival in a long-term national catastrophe. Modern conventional farming relies on power. You need power for machines, power for processing equipment and power for irrigation systems. It also relies on a lot of water and fertilizer (and pesticides). All aspects and resources required for modern conventional farming will be challenged during a long-term loss of the electrical grid. Going back to what more resembles 19th-century farming methods is likely a necessary outcome. But this comes with obvious disadvantages, not the least of which is increased labor requirements (humans replacing machines) and decreased production. One solution to consider is a "technology" that has been around for hundreds of years but has only recently garnered renewed attention: Aquaponics.

Using aquaponics in food production offers many solutions. If a civil defense organization advocates for small-scale aquaponics systems in schools and homes (and plans for larger-scale operations) prior to a catastrophe, this will go a long way towards increased food preparedness. In a nutshell, aquaponics requires only a fraction of the water of conventional farming, does not require fertilizer or pesticides and can be completely powered by solar or wind. If done right, aquaponics systems can be used to produce a large amount of food year-round with minimal power, water and labor.

The purpose of this chapter is to provide a quick introduction to aquaponics and some quick reference material that I have found useful (and that will be critical in a long-term power outage).

For detailed information, one of the best books on aquaponics is available for free as a technical paper from the Food and Agriculture Organization (FAO) of the United Nations. The book is called *Small-scale aquaponics food production: Integrated fish and plant farming* and is available as a .pdf file for download.[66] I recommend that the civil defense organization have several printed copies of the complete publication (288 pages) and also make multiple copies of "Appendix 8–Step-by-step guide to constructing small-scale aquaponics systems." These can be used for education and outreach both before and after a long-term catastrophe. This free U.N. publication is so detailed that it is literally the only reference you need for aquaponics. (Of course, for us Americans, we also need metric conversion charts, so I have provided those here along with some other quick reference charts.)

What is Aquaponics?

Aquaponics is the combination of hydroponics (growing plants without soil) and aquaculture (raising fish) to create a complete and symbiotic ecosystem. In aquaponics, the fish produce fertilizer for the plants and the plants clean the water for the fish. The only input into the system is fish food.

The system takes advantage of a natural symbiotic relationship between the three components: fish, beneficial bacteria, and plants as illustrated in the chart below.

---

66 Can be found at http://www.fao.org/publications/card/en/c/90bb6bfe-1ac3-4280-857e-1c5a20404b38/ (accessed August 3, 2017) or at http://livefreeaquaponicsllc.com (accessed August 3, 2017).

Aquaponics Cycle

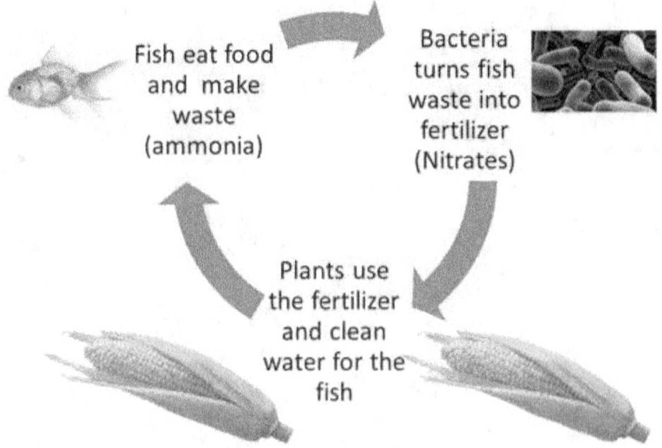

I know what you're thinking. "Oh my goodness, that is brilliant." Well, it is. It is what occurs every day in nature, and has been occurring before the first person walked the Earth. All aquaponics does is make "gardening" better by using this symbiotic relationship for the benefit of all. (We apparently thought for years that we could improve on nature—it seems that we really couldn't!)

Two angles on a typical indoor (basement) aquaponics system.

Aquaponics offers a great many advantages over conventional farming (or gardening):

- It is sustainable.
- Produces higher yields than conventional farming.
- Faster plant growth than conventional farming.
- Requires substantially less labor than conventional farming.
- Requires only a fraction of the energy of conventional farming.
- Produces both plants (fruits and vegetables) and fish for food.
- Requires only a fraction of the water of conventional farming.
- Indoor or greenhouse systems can be productive year-round.
- Produces its own fertilizer.
- Does not require soil.
- Creates little or no waste.

- Eliminates soil-borne diseases and pests.
- Can be completely organic (just use organic seeds and fish food).
- Can be used in areas with non-arable land.
- Systems can be made from a variety of commonly available materials.

If the system is built correctly, it can take advantage of gravity to move water through much of the system. Some energy is required, but solar and wind power can provide this energy, making aquaponics a viable solution for off-grid food production.

How Aquaponics Works

Broken down to its simplest components, here is how an aquaponics system works.

1. You feed the fish.
2. The fish produce waste.
3. Beneficial bacteria turn the fish waste into plant food.
4. The plants clean the water by using the food.
5. Clean water is returned to the fish.
6. The cycle repeats.

In this symbiotic system, the fish, bacteria, and plants all work to benefit each other. As long as the system remains in balance, it can produce a large amount of food regularly and sustainably. The only input to the system is the fish food.

Since the water is recycled through the system, very little is used compared to conventional farming. A small amount of water is used by the plants (transpiration) and a small amount is lost to the atmosphere (evaporation). However, aquaponics uses only a small fraction of the water used in conventional farming.

After a one-time capital and labor investment to build a system, aquaponics requires very little money and labor to maintain. A running aquaponics system requires no weeding, watering and other typical maintenance of conventional farming methods. In a running system, the only expense is fish food and a small amount of electricity—and if you produce your own fish food and run your system on solar power, you can reduce or eliminate these costs.

Aquaponics solves the inherent problems with aquaculture (the need to constantly dispose of fish waste) and hydroponics (the need to constantly add fertilizer to the growing solution). By merging the two systems, aquaponics makes the "problem" in each system the solution for the other system.

For an outdoor or greenhouse system, the only energy requirement may be for the water pump (and perhaps heating in the winter depending on the climate). For an indoor system, you would need energy for grow lights.

The basement aquaponics system pictured above runs on one submersible 1000 gph pump (92 watts) and six LED grow lights (19 watts each). Assuming you run the pump 24 hours per day and the grow lights for 16 hours per day, the system will use 4032 watts per day. This could be easily provided by a small off-grid solar power system, or a hybrid solar-wind system or generator. In a greenhouse, eliminating the LED lights, the pump would use 2208 watts per day, needing an even smaller solar power system.

Ideally, if a family has a small off-grid solar power system sized to run their well-pump and basement aquaponics garden, this contributes to both food and water security!

Types of Aquaponics Systems

There are three common types of aquaponics systems. Design differences in each type are limited only by the imagination of the builder. Some people have systems that employ any combination of the three types. The three most common types are media bed systems, deep water culture (DWC or "raft") systems and nutrient film technique (NFT) systems. The free United Nations FAO publication *Small-scale aquaponics food production* has detailed information on the three types of systems.

Between the three common systems, there is a great deal of versatility and scalability. Size can range from a small, family-run system in a basement or small backyard greenhouse to large commercial aquaponics farms capable of producing a great deal of food. Systems can be built ad-hoc from many locally-available materials.

Aquaponics in Civil Defense

There are a lot of reasons to consider the role of aquaponics in the civil defense context. One of the biggest challenges we face is the long-term disruption in the community's food supply. Aquaponics offers a flexible, scalable and year-round food production method that could substantially contribute to a community's resilience before an event and, ultimately, contribute substantially to a community's survival after an event.

The more people in the community who are knowledgeable in various methods of food production—including aquaponics—the better. Aquaponics can help make a community more food independent and therefore more resilient. Teaching food production techniques and food independence is a great outreach opportunity for the civil defense organization. Also, encouraging the use of alternative energy for the aquaponics systems (such as a small off-grid solar power system), will increase food independence from the power grid. Consideration should be given to using low-wattage LED grow lights and systems that require little or no heating for the fish.

The best types of fish and crops will vary depending on the local conditions and the area of the country. In some areas, people successfully run outdoor aquaponics systems year-round. In other areas, the system may need to be indoors or in a greenhouse.[67] For colder areas of the country, an indoor aquaponics system can provide a year-round food source.

---

67 I live in New Hampshire which gets real friggin' cold. However, my basement never gets below 52 degrees in the winter and never above 74 degrees in the summer. This range is perfect for rainbow trout, koi, goldfish and other coldwater fish. In the winter, I adjust my plants to cold weather varieties, such as broccoli, cauliflower, radishes, and leafy greens. I grow vegetables and fish all year long.

Charts and References

Below are some critical quick-references in both building and maintaining aquaponics systems.

CHART 1. WATER QUALITY TOLERANCES FOR THE ORGANISMS IN AQUAPONICS

Component	Water Temp (°F)	pH	Ammonia NH_3 (mg/liter)	Nitrite NO_2 (mg/liter)	Nitrate NO_3 (mg/liter)	Dissolved Oxygen (mg/liter)
Fish (warmwater)	72-90	6-8.5	< 3	< 1	< 400	4-6
Fish (coldwater)	50-64	6-8.5	< 1	< 0.1	< 400	6-8
Plants	61-86	5.5-7.5	< 30	< 1	-	> 3
Bacteria	57-93	6-8.5	< 3	< 1	-	4-8

Therefore, the best compromise is:

Component	Water Temp (°F)	pH	Ammonia NH_3 (mg/liter)	Nitrite NO_2 (mg/liter)	Nitrate NO_3 (mg/liter)	Dissolved Oxygen (mg/liter)
All	64-86	6-7	< 1	< 1	5-150	> 5

Source: Food and Agriculture Organization (FAO) of the United Nations.[68]

Note: Milligrams per liter (mg/liter or mg/l) is equal to parts per million (ppm). Some of the water test kits use ppm and some use mg/l. They are the same.

---

68 Food and Agriculture Organization (FAO) of the United Nations. *Small-scale aquaponics food production: Integrated fish and plant farming.* 2014. http://www.fao.org/publications/card/en/c/90bb6bfe-1ac3-4280-857e-1c5a20404b38/ (accessed September 11, 2017).

CHART 2. ADJUSTING pH

To Adjust pH	Use
↓ Down	**Distilled or Rainwater:** Adding distilled water (which has a pH of 7) or rainwater (which tends to have an even lower pH, perhaps 5-6) to the system can "dilute" the pH down. **Phosphoric acid (H_3PO_4):** Add to a separate reservoir of water and then add the treated water to the system. This also provides phosphorus for the plants.
↑ Up	**Natural calcium sources:** Use crushed seashells, crushed eggshells, coarse limestone grit or crushed chalk. Put the material in a porous bag suspended in the sump tank. Monitor pH every few days. **Calcium carbonate ($CaCO_3$):** Add a small amount at a time (1 teaspoon) and check the pH the next day. This also provides calcium for the plants. **Potassium carbonate (K_2CO_3):** Add a small amount at a time (1 teaspoon) and check the pH the next day. This also provides potassium for the plants.

Note: Over time, the nitrification process will lower the pH naturally. Be patient if it is a new system and running a slightly high pH.

CHART 3. NUTRIENTS NEEDED FOR PLANT GROWTH

Note: Nutrients followed by asterisks (*) are those that may need to be supplemented in aquaponics systems. (Adding K and Ca can affect pH, so be careful and go slowly.)

Macronutrients	Micronutrients
N—Nitrogen	Cl—Chorine
K—Potassium* (add potassium carbonate)	Fe—Iron* (add DPTA chelated iron)
Ca—Calcium* (add calcium carbonate)	Mn—Manganese
Mg—Magnesium	B—Boron
P—Phosphorus	Zn—Zinc
S—Sulfur	Cu—Copper
	Mo—Molybdenum

Source: New Mexico State University Cooperative Extension Service.[69]

---

69 Sallenave, Rossana. *Circular 680 Important Water Quality Parameters in aquaponics Systems.* New Mexico State University Cooperative Extension Service. http://aces.nmsu.edu/pubs/_circulars/CR680.pdf (accessed August 5, 2017).

NOTES:

Instead of potassium carbonate (K_2CO_3) you can use potassium hydroxide (KOH), but potassium hydroxide is much stronger than potassium carbonate.

Instead of calcium carbonate ($CaCO_3$) you can use calcium hydroxide ($Ca(OH)_2$), but calcium hydroxide is much stronger than calcium carbonate.

Dosages for added nutrients:

DPTA chelated iron: with a 10% powder, add 1/2 of a tablespoon (1 ½ teaspoons) per 100 gallons of water every 3 weeks.

Potassium carbonate: Adds potassium but lowers the pH. Add a small amount at a time (1 teaspoon) and check the pH the next day.

Calcium carbonate: Adds calcium but lowers the pH. Add a small amount at a time (1 teaspoon) and check the pH the next day.

Phosphoric acid: Adds phosphorus (which the plants like) but also raises the pH. Add a small amount to a separate reservoir of water, and then add the treated water to the system.

CHART 4. MAXIMUM FISH STOCKING DENSITY

	Maximum Fish	**Per Size of Tank**
Metric	10-20 kilograms	1000 liters
Standard	22-44 pounds	264 gallons

The recommended maximum stocking density for fish is 10–20 kg of fish per 1000 liters of water. For us stubborn folk, the above chart converts this into "American." If you are not harvesting the fish and keeping fish that can live for decades (like koi and goldfish), this becomes easy once the fish are full grown. If you are harvesting fish for food and restocking, you will need to stagger your harvests and stocking in such a way as not to throw the system off balance (i.e., don't harvest all your full-grown fish and replace them with small fingerlings at the same time).

CHART 5. FISH TYPES AND CHARACTERISTICS

Coldwater Fish (40-65°F)

Fish	Temp Range (°F)	Optimum Temp (°F)	Edible	Diet
Salmon	40-60	45-50	Yes	Carnivore
Brook trout	34-72	45-60	Yes	Carnivore
Rainbow trout	44-65	55-65	Yes	Carnivore
Brown trout	44-75	55-65	Yes	Carnivore

Coolwater Fish (65-75 °F)

Fish	Temp Range (°F)	Optimum Temp (°F)	Edible	Diet
Koi	45-90	65-75	No	Omnivore
Goldfish	45-90	65-75	No	Omnivore
Walleye	60-85	65-75	Yes	Carnivore
Yellow perch	60-85	68-74	Yes	Carnivore

Warmwater Fish (75-90 °F)

Fish	Temp Range (°F)	Optimum Temp (°F)	Edible	Diet
Crappie	35-90	55-80	Yes	Carnivore
Bluegill	39-90	60-80	Yes	Omnivore
Channel catfish	33-95	70-85	Yes	Omnivore
Smallmouth bass	50-73	75-86	Yes	Carnivore
Largemouth bass	50-80	75-86	Yes	Carnivore
Pumpkinseed	62-88	75-89	Yes	Omnivore
Carp	40-93	77-86	Some	Omnivore
Barramundi	64-93	79-84	Yes	Carnivore
Nile tilapia	57-97	80-86	Yes	Omnivore

Various sources, including: Purdue University Extension,[70] University of Illinois at Urbana-Champaign,[71] Ohio State University Extension,[72] University of California, Davis,[73] Food and Agriculture Organization (FAO) of the United Nations.[74] Note that the data varies dramatically between sources.

---

70 Swann, LaDon. *A Fish Farmer's Guide to Understanding Water Quality.* Department of Animal Sciences Illinois-Indiana Sea Grant Program, Purdue University. https://www.extension.purdue.edu/extmedia/as/as-503.html (accessed August 5, 2017).

71 Hinz, Leon C, Metzke, Brian A., Holtrop, Ann Marie. *Evaluating Water Temperature, Habitat and Fish Communities in Candidate Coolwater Streams in Illinois.* University of Illinois at Urbana-Champaign
Prairie Research Institute. https://www.dnr.illinois.gov/conservation/iwap/documents/coolwater-streams.pdf (accessed August 5, 2017).

72 Lynch, William Jr. *Fish Species Selection for Aquaponics.* Ohio State University Extension. http://ohioaquaculture.org/pdf/FishSpeciesSelectionAquaponics.pdf (accessed August 5, 2017).

73 *Species Selection for Recreational Fishing in Small Ponds and Lakes.* University of California, Davis. Department of Animal Science. http://aqua.ucdavis.edu/DatabaseRoot/pdf/ASAQ-C13.PDF (accessed August 5, 2017).

74 Food and Agriculture Organization (FAO) of the United Nations. Small-scale aquaponics food production: Integrated fish and plant farming. 2014. http://www.fao.org/publications/card/en/c/90bb6bfe-1ac3-4280-857e-1c5a20404b38/ (accessed September 11, 2017).

CHART 6. PLANT TYPES AND CHARACTERISTICS

Cool Season Plants (40-75°F)

Plant	Optimum Air Temp Range (°F)	Minimum Soil Temp (°F)	Growth Time to Harvest
Arugula	50-65	40	21-30 days
Beets	60-65	40	55-80 days
Broccoli	56-65	40	60-100 days
Brussels sprouts	45-75	60	90-180 days
Cabbage	59-68	20	45-70 days
Carrots	60-65	45-85	60-80 days
Cauliflower	68-77	60	60-90 days
Celery	60-65	60	90-140 days
Chives	40-85	65	80 days
Collards	60-65	40	70-80 days
Kale	60-65	40	65-75 days
Leeks	55-75	65-75	85-150 days
Lettuce	59-72	40	24-32 days
Parsley	59-77	70	80 days
Parsnips	40-70	50	80-120 days
Peas	60-79	40-55	50-110 days
Potatoes	60-65	40	100-115 days
Radish	60-65	40	25-50 days
Scallions	55-75	40	60-120 days
Spinach	35-75	40	60-65 days
Swiss Chard	40-80	50	25-35 days
Turnips	60-65	50	35-50 days
Winter Squash	65-75	60	70-120 days

Warm Season Plants (75-100°F)

Plant	Optimum Air Temp Range (°F)	Minimum Soil Temp (°F)	Growth Time to Harvest
Basil	68-77	70	45 days
Beans	70-80	60	50-110 days
Corn	60-75	60	70-100 days
Cucumbers	65-83	60	55-65 days
Eggplant	60-85	65	90-120 days
Melons	80-100	50	80-125 days
Okra	70-85	60	50-60 days
Peppers	58-86	60	60-95 days
Summer squash	65-75	60	45-75 days
Sweet Potatoes	70-85	65	150-170 days
Tomatoes	70-85	60	50-70 days

Sources: *United Nations*, FAO Fisheries and Aquaculture[75], Penn State University Extension[76], Oregon State University Extension[77]

Note: While aquaponics does not use "soil" the minimum soil temperature is instructive when planning which plants will grow best in the water temperatures encountered in your system.

75 *Small-scale aquaponic food production. Integrated fish and plant farming.* United Nations, FAO Fisheries and Aquaculture Technical Paper No. 589. http://www.fao.org/3/a-i4021e/i4021e06.pdf (accessed August 5, 2017).

76 *Vegetable Planting and Transplanting Guide.* PennState Extension. http://extension.psu.edu/plants/gardening/fact-sheets/vegetable-gardening/vegetable-guide (accessed August 5, 2017).

77 *Is it time to plant vegetables? Ask your soil thermometer.* Oregon State University Extension. http://extension.oregonstate.edu/gardening/it-time-plant-vegetables-ask-your-soil-thermometer (accessed August 5, 2017).

CHART 7. METRIC CONVERSION: TEMPERATURE

Celsius	Fahrenheit	Celsius	Fahrenheit
0	32	50	122
1	33.8	51	123.8
2	35.6	52	125.6
3	37.4	53	127.4
4	39.2	54	129.2
5	41	55	131
6	42.8	56	132.8
7	44.6	57	134.6
8	46.4	58	136.4
9	48.2	59	138.2
10	50	60	140
11	51.8	61	141.8
12	53.6	62	143.6
13	55.4	63	145.4
14	57.2	64	147.2
15	59	65	149
16	60.8	66	150.8
17	62.6	67	152.6
18	64.4	68	154.4
19	66.2	69	156.2
20	68	70	158
21	69.8	71	159.8
22	71.6	72	161.6
23	73.4	73	163.4
24	75.2	74	165.2
25	77	75	167
26	78.8	76	168.8
27	80.6	77	170.6
28	82.4	78	172.4
29	84.2	79	174.2
30	86	80	176

Celsius	Fahrenheit	Celsius	Fahrenheit
31	87.8	81	177.8
32	89.6	82	179.6
33	91.4	83	181.4
34	93.2	84	183.2
35	95	85	185
36	96.8	86	186.8
37	98.6	87	188.6
38	100.4	88	190.4
39	102.2	89	192.2
40	104	90	194
41	105.8	91	195.8
42	107.6	92	197.6
43	109.4	93	199.4
44	111.2	94	201.2
45	113	95	203
46	114.8	96	204.8
47	116.6	97	206.6
48	118.4	98	208.4
49	120.2	99	210.2
		100	212

CHART 8. METRIC CONVERSION: LIQUID

Liter	Quart
0.25	0.264
0.5	0.528
0.75	0.793
1	1.057
2	2.113
3	3.170
4	4.227
5	5.283
6	6.340
7	7.397
8	8.454
9	9.510
10	10.567
50	52.834
100	105.669
1000	1056.688

Quart	Liter	
0.25	0.237	(cup)
0.5	0.473	
0.75	0.710	
1	0.946	(quart)
2	1.893	
3	2.839	
4	3.785	(gallon)
5	4.732	
6	5.678	
7	6.624	
8	7.571	
9	8.517	
10	9.464	
50	47.318	
100	94.635	
1000	946.353	

CHART 9. METRIC CONVERSION: WEIGHT

Gram	Ounce	
1	0.035	
2	0.071	
3	0.106	
4	0.141	
5	0.176	
6	0.212	
7	0.247	
8	0.282	
9	0.317	
10	0.353	
16	0.564	
20	0.705	
50	1.764	
100	3.527	
1000	35.274	(kilogram)
2000	70.548	

Ounce	Gram	
1	28.350	
2	56.699	
3	85.049	
4	113.398	
5	141.748	
6	170.097	
7	198.447	
8	226.796	
9	255.146	
10	283.495	
16	453.592	(pound)
20	566.990	
50	1417.476	
100	2834.952	
1000	28349.523	
2000	56699.046	(ton)

CHART 10. METRIC CONVERSION: MEASUREMENTS

Centimeter	Inch	
1	0.394	
2	0.787	
3	1.181	
4	1.575	
5	1.969	
6	2.362	
7	2.756	
8	3.150	
9	3.543	
10	3.937	
12	4.724	
24	9.449	
36	14.173	
100	39.370	(meter)
1,000	393.701	

Inch	Centimeter	
1	2.54	
2	5.08	
3	7.62	
4	10.16	
5	12.7	
6	15.24	
7	17.78	
8	20.32	
9	22.86	
10	25.4	
12	30.48	(foot)
24	60.96	
36	91.44	(yard)
100	254	
1,000	2,540	

Millimeter	Inch	
1	0.03937	
2	0.07874	
3	0.11811	
4	0.15748	
5	0.19685	
6	0.23622	
7	0.275591	
8	0.314961	
9	0.354331	
10	0.393701	(centimeter)
11	0.433071	
12	0.472441	
100	3.937008	
1,000	39.3701	(meter)

Inch	Millimeter	
1	25.4	
2	50.8	
3	76.2	
4	101.6	
5	127	
6	152.4	
7	177.8	
8	203.2	
9	228.6	
10	254	
11	279.4	
12	304.8	(foot)
100	2,540	
1,000	25,400	

Metric to Standard

1 millimeter (mm)	=	0.03937 inches
1 centimeter (cm)	=	0.39370 inches
1 meter (m)	=	39.37008 inches
1 meter (m)	=	3.28084 feet
1 meter (m)	=	1.09361 yards
1 kilometer (km)	=	1093.6133 yards
1 kilometer (km)	=	0.62137 miles

Standard to Metric

1 inch	=	2.54 centimeters (cm)
1 foot	=	30.48 centimeters (cm)
1 yard	=	91.44 centimeters (cm)
1 yard	=	0.9144 meters (m)
1 mile	=	1609.344 meters (m)
1 mile	=	1.609344 kilometers (km)

Nine

Is Emergency Management Ready for a Long-Term Blackout?

Is Emergency Management in the U.S.—and in your community—prepared for a long-term loss of the electric grid?

Here is FEMA's definition of Emergency Management: it is the managerial function charged with creating the framework within which communities reduce vulnerability to hazards and cope with disasters. Emergency Management protects communities by coordinating and integrating all activities necessary to build, sustain, and improve the capability to mitigate, prepare for, respond to, and recover from threatened or actual natural disasters, acts of terrorism, or other man-made disasters.

That is a good mouthful of *federalspeak* for "the people holding the (mostly empty) bag when the grid goes down."

One of the strengths of modern Emergency Management is its flexibility. Most towns can handle a structure fire or an auto accident with their own resources. But when something larger happens, like a tornado or a fiery multi-car pile-up with multiple casualties, the system expands and resources are brought in from neighboring towns. And in a larger-scale disaster, like a hurricane or earthquake, resources can be brought in from the federal government and agencies all over the state or country. So, in theory (and in practice), Emergency Management can handle disasters small and large.

But this strength is also a critical weakness: What if the disaster was of national-scale and therefore no outside resources available to help your town? What if you were on your own?

There have been several recent articles of note, including an article in *Fire Engineering* by Ken Chrosniak: "Electric Power Blackout: The Power of One."[78] Another good article to read is by Garrison Wells: "Threat of Massive Grid Shutdown Increasing in Face of Disasters."[79] And more recently, Eric Holdeman has blogged about electromagnetic pulse in *Emergency Management Magazine* online.[80] If you are an emergency manager, you really need to read these articles: You and your jurisdiction are not prepared for a long-term blackout.

So let's do a quick tabletop exercise.

Scenario: A massive solar flare (coronal mass ejection) has taken down the majority of the electric grid in the United States. Many of the extra-high-voltage (EHV) transformers have been damaged and it may be months—or longer—before power is restored. All you have is whatever resources your town or jurisdiction currently has on hand (disasters are, after all, "come as you are"). If you want to spice it up, assume this is in the worst season for your area, e.g., winter in New England or summer in Texas. Because this is a national-scale disaster, you can't count on any aid from the outside for the foreseeable future—perhaps months. The cavalry is not coming.

Exercise Objectives: (Oh, I forgot to mention, you're going to fail this exercise and half the population or more of your town will die—but that's okay. This is only a drill. The purpose of a drill is to harvest the lessons learned and do better next time—or when it happens for real. The vast majority of towns, states and even the federal government have never drilled this scenario.)

---

78 http://www.fireengineering.com/articles/2013/07/electric-power-blackout-the-power-of-one.html (accessed August 6, 2017).

79 http://gazette.com/apocalypse-threat-of-massive-grid-shutdown-increasing-in-face-of-terrorism-natural-disasters/article/1509048 (accessed August 6, 2017).

80 http://www.govtech.com/em/emergency-blogs/disaster-zone/theemphazard.html   (accessed August 6, 2017).

The objectives are:

1. Determine what resources and capabilities you have.
2. Determine the obvious problems your town/jurisdiction will face.
3. Think about things that could be done prior to an event to prepare and mitigate.

The first objective is fairly simple. You probably already have a good idea of what your town's resources are. But, your existing resources and capabilities may be less than you think. Will all your resources show up to work if their families are in jeopardy from a national catastrophe? Also, even if most of them do, remember that all you have is what you have in town now: fuel, medical supplies, number of cops and firemen, etc. Nothing else is available.

For the second objective, I'm not even going to throw in any injects. The facts are bad enough. When the grid goes down for a long period of time, we can briefly broad-brush the challenges to a town as follows:

- Long-term interruption of power
  - People will be without heat/AC.
  - People will be without refrigeration.
  - People will be without the ability to perform basic things like cooking or boiling water.
  - People will be without basic sanitation and, hence, at risk for diseases.
  - People may be without transportation immediately (EMP damage) or soon (lack of fuel).
  - Most, if not all, forms of communication will be disrupted.
  - Critical backup generators will soon run out of fuel.
- Long-term interruption of supply chain
  - Food delivery will stop.
  - Fuel delivery will stop.
  - Delivery of medicine and medical supplies to pharmacies and hospitals will stop.
  - Delivery of all products, parts and supplies will stop.

- Long-term interruption of essential services
  - o Water service will stop.
  - o Sewer service will stop.
  - o Fire, EMS, and police will be unable to respond (for lack of fuel, personnel and communications).
  - o Medical services will be severely disrupted or unavailable.
- Collapse of law and order (temporary or permanent)
  - o The police will not have the manpower, communications, or transportation to provide security for the community.
  - o Desperate people will resort to looting, burglary, robbery, or any means necessary to get food and water.
  - o It is unlikely that federal help is "on the way" any time soon.
  - o Many local governments will quickly become ineffective.
- Starving refugees arriving from urban areas
  - o Even if, miraculously, you live in a community that is prepared and has a plan to attack the above challenges, look to your nearest urban areas—refugees will soon be forced to flee the cities. Any plan for a town's survival will have to address how to humanely handle desperate refugees while protecting the town and maintaining law and order.
  - o Town borders will have to be monitored and protected.
  - o Town assets will have to be guarded from looters/criminals.

When you really think about the implications of each of the items above—and begin to put this operating picture together, it is grim. And, local Emergency Management will be holding the bag. Nobody higher is coming in to become the incident commander. The National Guard can't come to every town (and they have their own problems—guardsman are going to have a tough choice when asked to report to duty when their families are in danger).

Let's take one of the above problems as an example: Desperate people will resort to looting, burglary, robbery, or any means necessary to get food and water.

So, you have a grocery store and a pharmacy in town. Those are going to quickly become targets. How many meals does the average family in your town (and neighboring towns) have in the cupboard? With the supply chain gone and no food coming in, what do you think will happen one week from now when people are out of food? This means you are X number of meals away from anarchy. Can your law enforcement resources handle this?

Let's look at another: Water service will stop.

Most people get water either from "city water" service or a well. Both require electricity. The vast majority of your town will be without their primary water supply. People are going to be at risk for waterborne diseases—if they are lucky enough to have even questionable water to drink.

As you go through and think about the implications of each of the above (and perhaps a few more that you may think of—the above list is not comprehensive) one thing becomes clear. When the size of the disaster overwhelms the local capabilities, Emergency Management's dependence on outside resources has failed us here. We need to be able to depend on ourselves in this worst-case national catastrophe scenario.

It is also clear that for any town or jurisdiction to adequately prepare, mitigate, respond and recover from a long-term electric grid outage, we need to do a lot of work beforehand. This brings us to the third objective: what could be done prior to an event to prepare and mitigate?

The answer is, a lot.

The answer is not "that could never happen" (because it could) or "if that happened, there is just no way to be prepared for it" (because that is just patently false). Several members of Congress have been concerned about this vulnerability of the electric grid for years and there are reams of Congressional testimony and federal reports that conclude that this can happen. Moreover, several members of Congress advocated in 2012 that communities start a civil defense program and be prepared to fend for themselves in the absence of federal assistance for a prolonged period of time.

It would be great if the federal government took concrete steps to protect the electric grid. Legislative attempts to do so have failed for years to make it out of committee. The companies that own and operate the electric grid are against such legislation—and they have a lot of money to lobby against it.

So, in the absence of the federal government taking steps to protect the grid, local Emergency Management must take steps to protect their towns—to prepare, mitigate, respond and recover from a national-scale long-term blackout. This scenario needs to be one of the hazards considered in our "all hazard" comprehensive approach.

Some initial suggested steps

1. Every town and jurisdiction should do a tabletop drill with a long-term national blackout scenario (months).
2. Nobody has a budget for this—you will need community involvement. Starting a Community Emergency Response Team (CERT) or involving your CERT if you have one, is a great way to start getting the community involved.
3. If you can get some public interest, consider starting a nonprofit civil defense organization that has this specific mission:
   (a) To educate and promote individual, family, and town preparedness for disasters;
   (b) To provide disaster assistance and relief to town residents in the event of a disaster; and
   (c) To educate and provide planning and resource options to the town for preparation and response to a "worst-case," long-term catastrophe affecting the town.

Some members of Congress attempted to pass a resolution advocating that communities and their citizens do this. While House Resolution 762 (112th Congress)[81] may have died in committee along with other legislation to protect the electric grid, a good idea does not need to pass Congress to be a good idea.

---

81 See Appendix 1 for the full test of the resolution, or get it from the Government Printing Office at: https://www.gpo.gov/fdsys/pkg/BILLS-112hres762ih/pdf/BILLS-112hres762ih.pdf (accessed August 6, 2017).

Is Emergency Management ready for a long-term blackout? You will have to answer this question for your own town or jurisdiction. After all, it will be local Emergency Management that owns this problem. It will be too late for you to figure it out once the lights go off.

What We Learn From Blackouts

"What we learn from history is that we do not learn from history."

I've always loved this quote from Benjamin Disraeli. But it occurs to me that perhaps what is more dangerous than **not learning** from history, **is learning** from history.

What most Americans have learned from their experiences with blackouts is quite dangerous: Our collective experience with blackouts is that they are temporary. The power will be back in a few hours (or days, at most) so all we need to do is wait it out. The power company will rescue us.

Maybe some of us are even "prepared" for a blackout and have a generator and some gas. Maybe we have 72 hours worth of canned food stored away like FEMA tells us. Even in the Emergency Management world, every exercise comes to an end. Every hurricane comes to an end. Every blackout comes to an end. Moreover, we have the "edge effect" where there are always resources available from outside the blackout area to assist us until the power comes back.

We are complacent. "Blackouts are temporary" we think.

But what if the power went off and did not come back for a year? While Congress has studied—and failed to act—on this scenario for years, more and more people in Emergency Management are thinking about a long-term blackout scenario.

There can be no serious debate that our electric grid is vulnerable to a number of things, from terrorist attack, cyber-attack, electromagnetic pulse weapon, solar flare to a good old-fashioned ice storm or errant tree branch. While a long-term failure is considered by some to be a remote possibility, the possibility is frightening. And now there is evidence that both Iran and North

Korea are actively pursuing electromagnetic pulse and cyber weapons with the specific purpose of taking down the U.S. electric grid.

Does anybody out there really think that they wouldn't do it? U.S. "retaliation" means little to either country. Taking out "the great Satan" (in Iran's case) would be worth whatever we sent back—so our usual deterrent strategy is not helpful here. There was an excellent article about this in the *Washington Times* by R. James Woolsey and Peter Vincent Pry: "When Iran goes nuclear: Failure to protect the nation would amount to dereliction of duty."[82]

Okay. Even if there was a massive grid outage, somebody would rescue us, right? Wrong. The United States is completely unprepared. The sad thing is, we don't have to be. Even if Congress fails to act, individual communities can do much to prepare for and mitigate such a scenario.

So, one of the most dangerous things we have learned from history is that blackouts are temporary events lasting hours or, at most, a few days. We are completely unprepared for a long-term national-scale blackout. Until we start thinking about it, the lives of millions of Americans remain in peril. September 11, 2001 would be just a minor incident on the scale compared to what a long-term national power outage would be.

But, it can start in your community. The federal government won't be there to rescue us in a long-term national blackout. We will have to rescue ourselves.

---

82 http://www.washingtontimes.com/news/2015/mar/2/r-james-woolsey-peter-vincent-pry-when-iran-goes-n/ (accessed August 13, 2017).

Appendix 1: House Resolution 762 (112th Congress)

[Note: This resolution was referred to committee and was never acted upon by the House.]

112th CONGRESS
2d Session
H. RES. 762

Expressing the sense of the House of Representatives regarding community-based civil defense and power generation.

IN THE HOUSE OF REPRESENTATIVES
August 2, 2012

Mr. BARTLETT (for himself, Mr. FRANKS of Arizona, Ms. CLARKE of New York, and Mr. JOHNSON of Georgia) submitted the following resolution; which was referred to the Committee on Transportation and Infrastructure.

RESOLUTION

Expressing the sense of the House of Representatives regarding community-based civil defense and power generation.

Whereas the United States has become increasingly more dependent on electronic delivery systems to power daily needs and provide for the common defense;

Whereas these systems would be rendered useless or their functions significantly reduced in the event of a 'high impact low-frequency' event such as a cyber attack, coordinated physical attack on electric grid and communications assets, or the electromagnetic pulse (EMP) effects of either a 100-year solar storm or high-altitude nuclear burst;

Whereas the 2010 North American Electric Reliability Corporation (NERC) report, 'High-Impact Low-Frequency Vulnerabilities to the Bulk American Power System,' discusses the wide range of threats that could disrupt, damage, or destroy sufficient amounts of the power grids to cause widespread death and economic disruption;

Whereas the January 2010 Federal Energy Regulatory Commission (FERC) report, 'Electromagnetic Pulse: Effects on the U.S. Power Grid,' provides detail into the vulnerability of power grids from the electromagnetic pulse (EMP) effects of extreme space weather and high-altitude nuclear effects and intentional electromagnetic interference;

Whereas the Congressional EMP Commission reports of 2004 and 2008 outline the interdependent nature of all critical infrastructure, especially to power and telecommunications and their vulnerability to the EMP effects of extreme space weather and high-altitude nuclear bursts;

Whereas the National Defense University hosted a series of workshops and an energy security exercise in October 2011 with broad participation of Federal, State, [and] local government, and the private sector highlighting the need for greater local sustainability in light of a prolonged nationwide power loss;

Whereas the Hoover-Brookings joint report on distributed power shows that the value of local power generation for security applications is either cost competitive or approaching competitiveness as new innovations come to market;

Whereas, on March 30, 2012, the United States Department of Homeland Security published the 'National Preparedness Report' (Report) seeking to create 'an all-of-nation' approach to preparedness;

Whereas the Federal Emergency Management Agency (FEMA) was assigned as the National Preparedness Report Coordinator, 'Efforts to improve national preparedness have incorporated the whole community, which includes individuals, communities, the private and nonprofit sectors, faith-based organizations, and Federal, State, local, tribal, and territorial governments;'

Whereas the 'National Preparedness Report' focuses on a catastrophic planning framework known as 'Maximums of Maximums,' which centers on collaborative, whole community planning for worst-case scenarios that exceed government capabilities and therefore focus on more local and individual efforts for survival and recovery;

Whereas these high-impact, low-frequency events would cause regional or nationwide collapse of critical infrastructure that could last months or longer, it is incumbent on the Federal Government to reassess its civilian civil defense strategies to include local governments and individual citizens; and

Whereas it is in the interest of national security and local community viability that every community and institution begin to reestablish its ability to generate at least 20 percent of its own power for its critical infrastructure and services in order to provide its citizens with food and water: Now, therefore, be it

Resolved, That the House of Representatives—

(1) encourages every community to develop its own 'civil defense program' working with citizens, leaders, and institutions ranging from local fire halls, schools, and faith-based organizations, to create sustainable local infrastructure and planning capacity so that it might mitigate high-impact scenarios and be better prepared to survive and recover from these worst-case disaster scenarios and be better able to affordably and sustainably meet the needs of the community in times of peace and tranquility;

(2) encourages every citizen to develop an individual emergency plan to prepare for the absence of government assistance for extended periods;

(3) encourages each local community to foster the capability of providing at least 20 percent of its own critical needs such as local power generation, food, and water, while protecting local infrastructure whenever possible from the threats that threaten centralized infrastructure, and

do so with the urgency and importance inherent in an all-of-nation civil defense program developed by citizens and their local communities; and

(4) encourages State governments and Federal agencies to support the ability of local communities to become stronger, self-reliant, and better able to assist neighboring communities in times of great need.

Appendix 2: Sample Civil Defense Organization

There is no one-size-fits-all method for starting an organization, so these documents should be taken as just "starting point examples" of a civil defense organization. Moreover, it is nearly impossible to draft template articles of incorporation and Bylaws that would meet the requirements of every state. Each state may have different requirements for incorporating as a nonprofit and for registering to solicit for charitable donations.[83] You should check with the secretary of state's office in your state and/or an attorney in your state for the specific requirements. Finally, to obtain tax-exempt status under Section 501(c)(3) of the Internal Revenue Code, an organization must file a Form 1023 with the IRS.

There are many different structures and options for governance. For example, a nonprofit may be structured with or without "members," and there are advantages and disadvantages to each.[84] Careful consideration should be given to the structure at the initial formation, as it can be difficult to change later.

These documents are presented simply to give you starting point ideas of what a mission statement, articles of incorporation, and Bylaws for a civil defense organization could look like.

---

83 For example, depending on the state, a nonprofit may be required to register to solicit charitable donations, either with the state attorney general, department of consumer protection or another state agency. Also it might be required to file papers with the state taxing authority.

84 Many attorneys may advise *against* structuring a nonprofit organization with members unless required by the state, or in the case of organizations that will have dues-paying members.

Sample Mission Statement #1[85]

The mission of the [Town Y] Civil Defense Corp. is to educate and promote individual, family, and town preparedness for disasters; to provide disaster assistance and relief to town residents in the event of a disaster; and to educate and provide planning and resource options to the town for preparation and response to a "worst-case," long-term catastrophe affecting the town.

Sample Mission Statement #2[86]

The mission of the [Town Y] Civil Defense Corp. is

- o To develop a civil defense program for [Town Y], working with citizens, leaders, and institutions ranging from local fire halls, schools, and faith-based organizations to create sustainable local infrastructure and planning capacity, so as to mitigate high-impact scenarios and be better prepared to survive and recover from these worst-case disaster scenarios;
- o To educate and encourage every citizen to develop an individual emergency plan to prepare for the absence of government assistance for extended periods;
- o To encourage the [Town Y] community to foster the capability of providing for its own critical needs, such as local power generation, food, and water in time of a worst-case disaster scenario; and
- o To educate and encourage [Town Y] residents and the [Town Y] government to become stronger, more self-reliant, and better able to assist neighboring communities in times of great need.

---

85 The mission statement should be imported *verbatim* into the articles of incorporation and bylaws.

86 This sample mission statement is adopted from the proposed House Resolution at Appendix 1.

Sample Charter

Articles of Incorporation of [Town Y] Civil Defense Corp.[87]

First: The name of the corporation shall be [Town Y] Civil Defense Corp. (the "Corporation").

Second: The place in this state where the principal office of the Corporation is to be located is the Town of [Town Y].

Third: The nature of the activities to be conducted or the purposes of the Corporation are to engage in any lawful act or activity permitted under the Nonprofit Corporation Law of [State], (the "Act") which is charitable, religious, educational and/or scientific in nature, entitling the Corporation to exemption from taxation under Section 501(c)(3) of the Internal Revenue Code of 1986, as the same may be amended and in force from time to time (the "Code"), and more particularly to:[88]

(a) To educate and promote individual, family, and town preparedness for disasters;

(b) To provide disaster assistance and relief to town residents in the event of a disaster; and

(c) To educate and provide planning and resource options to the town for preparation and response to a "worst-case," long-term catastrophe affecting the town.

Fourth: The names and addresses of the persons who are the initial directors of the corporation are as follows:

---

87 In some states "certificate of incorporation," in other states "articles of incorporation."

88 The mission statement should be imported *verbatim* into the articles of incorporation and bylaws.

Name _________________________ Address_____________________________

Name _________________________ Address_____________________________

Name _________________________ Address_____________________________

Fifth: All the assets and earnings of the Corporation shall be used exclusively for its exempt purposes, including the payment of expenses incidental thereto. No part of any net earnings shall inure to the benefit of any employee of the Corporation or be distributed to its Directors, Officers, or any private person, except that the Corporation shall be empowered to pay reasonable compensation for services rendered and make payments and distributions in furtherance of the purposes set forth in Article II of these Bylaws. Notwithstanding any other provision of these Bylaws, the Corporation will not carry on any activities not permitted by an organization exempt under Section 501(c)(3) of the Code, or the corresponding provision of any future federal law, or organizations whose contributions which are exempt under Section 170(c)(2) of the Code, or the corresponding provision of any future federal law. The Corporation shall have no capital stock, pay no dividends, distribute no part of its net income or assets to any Directors, Officers, and private property of the subscribers, Directors or Officers shall not be liable for the debts of the Corporation. No substantial part of the Corporation's activity shall be for the carrying on of a campaign of propaganda or otherwise attempting to influence legislation. The Corporation shall not participate in any political campaign and will not engage in political campaigns or attempt to influence legislation or interfere with any political campaign on behalf of or in opposition to any candidate for public office.

[If reference to federal law in articles of incorporation imposes a limitation that is invalid in your state, you may wish to substitute the following for the last sentence of the preceding paragraph: "Notwithstanding any other provision of these articles, this corporation shall not, except to an insubstantial degree, engage in any activities or exercise any powers that are not in furtherance of the purposes of this corporation."]

Sixth: Upon dissolution of the Corporation, the Board of Directors shall, after paying or making provision for payment of all liabilities of the Corporation, including the costs and expenses of such dissolution, distribute all assets for one or more exempt purposes within the meaning of section 501(c)(3) of the Internal Revenue Code, or the corresponding section of any future federal tax code, or shall be distributed to the federal government, or to a state or local government, for a public purpose. Any such assets not so disposed of shall be disposed of by a court of competent Jurisdiction of the county in which the principal office of the corporation is then located, exclusively for such purposes or to such organization or organizations, as said Court shall determine, which are organized and operated exclusively for such purposes.

In witness whereof, we have hereunto subscribed our names this ____ day of 20______.

Signatures of initial directors.

Note: The IRS has a sample charter for a 501(c)(3) organization on their website.[89] The IRS sample charter will meet the standards for the IRS—but be sure it also meets any additional requirements of your state. The IRS sample is missing provisions that many attorneys may recommend be included. Some additional common provisions include:

1. Some states require that the articles of incorporation specify whether or not the corporation has members.
2. For a non-member corporation, a statement may be included that the corporation shall operate under the management of a self-perpetuating board of directors.
3. A provision prohibiting campaign activity and limiting lobbying may be included.
4. A provision regarding private foundation restrictions may be included.
5. A provision regarding the standards for amending the certificate of incorporation may be included.
6. States vary in the treatment of liability and indemnification of directors. In some states this can be affected by what is stated (or not stated) in the articles of incorporation.
7. Some states have volunteer protection statutes, which may also be referenced.

---

89 http://www.irs.gov/Charities-&-Non-Profits/Charitable-Organizations/Sample-Organizing-Documents-Public-Charity (accessed September 11, 2017).

Bylaws (Sample #1: Without Members)

BYLAWS OF [Town Y] Civil Defense Corp.[90]

ARTICLE I
Name, Office, and Duration

1. Name. The name of this corporation is [Town Y] Civil Defense Corp.
2. Location. The principle place of business and administrative office shall be located at [address].
3. Duration. The Corporation shall have perpetual existence.

ARTICLE II
Purpose

1. The nature of the activities to be conducted or the purposes of the Corporation are to engage in any lawful act or activity permitted under the Nonprofit Corporation Law of [State], (the "Act") which is charitable, religious, educational and/or scientific in nature, entitling the Corporation to exemption from taxation under Section 501(c)(3) of the Internal Revenue Code of 1986, as the same may be amended and in force from time to time (the "Code"), and more particularly:
   (a) To educate and promote individual, family, and town preparedness for disasters;
   (b) To provide disaster assistance and relief to town residents in the event of a disaster; and
   (c) To educate and provide planning and resource options to the town for preparation and response to a "worst-case," long-term catastrophe affecting the town.

---

90 It is critical to consult your state's laws and/or an attorney when drafting bylaws as different states have different requirements.

ARTICLE III
Membership[91]

1. The Corporation shall have no members.

ARTICLE IV
Board of Directors

1. Election and Term of Office.[92] The members of the initial Board of Directors of the Corporation shall be those individuals named in the Articles of Incorporation and shall serve until their successors are elected. The members of the Board of Directors shall be elected by the Directors at the annual meeting of the Board of Directors. Members of the Board of Directors shall serve for one-year renewable terms.
2. Number. The initial number of Directors shall be three (3) and may be increased or decreased without further amendment of these Bylaws. At no time may the number of Directors be less than three (3).
3. Qualifications.[93] To serve as a Director, an individual shall be a current resident, property owner, business operator, or employee of the town and shall have one or more of the following qualifications:
    (a) Prior experience serving on a nonprofit board
    (b) Law enforcement training and experience
    (c) Military training and experience
    (d) Fire, EMS, or Emergency Management training and experience
    (e) Medical training and experience

---

91 Some states also require this in the articles of incorporation.

92 The initial Directors should be elected as part of the incorporation process, either in the certificate of incorporation or in a "consent" signed by the incorporator(s). An alternative to 1 year terms would be staggered or classified terms. A common method is three-year staggered terms, with the possibility that 1/3 of the Board rotates off in any given year.

93 Some attorneys may suggest taking this enumeration of qualifications out of the bylaws and instead put them into a Board Manual. This way, there is flexibility to bring someone onto the Board who doesn't fit any of these criteria but may serve another purpose, without violating the bylaws or opening up a dispute about a Directors' qualifications.

(f) General business or entrepreneurial experience

(g) Training and experience in specific skill sets sought by the Board

and shall have a desire to use his or her knowledge, skills and resources to help the town to survive and recover from worst-case disaster scenarios.

4. Powers. The Board of Directors shall have all corporate authority, except such powers as are otherwise provided in these Bylaws and the laws of the State of _______, to conduct the affairs of the Corporation in accordance with these Bylaws. The Board of Directors may, by general resolution, delegate to committees of their own number or to officers of the Corporation such powers as they deem appropriate.

5. Regular Meetings. Regular meetings of the Board of Directors shall be held at the place and time designated by the Board of Directors, including phone conference calls, and monthly or annual meetings, or otherwise called by a majority of the Board of Directors.

6. Special Meetings. Special meetings may be called by the President of the Corporation or a majority of the Board of Directors. Persons authorized to call special meetings shall provide written notice of the time and location of such meetings and state the purpose thereof, and no other matter shall be considered by the Board of Directors at such special meeting except upon unanimous vote of all Directors present. At least two days advance notice is required for special meetings.

7. Annual Meetings. Directors may meet each year for the purpose of organization, the election of officers, and transaction of other business. The time and location of such meeting shall be noticed in writing.

8. Notice and Waiver. Notice of regular meetings need not be in writing. Attendance at any meeting shall be considered waiver of the notice requirement thereof.

9. Quorum. A majority of the Directors then in office shall constitute a quorum for the transaction of business at any meeting of the Board of Directors. A majority vote of a quorum present at a meeting is

required for any action by the Board. Any amendment to the Bylaws requires a majority vote all directors then in office.

10. Vacancy. Any vacancy occurring in the Board of Directors shall be filled by majority vote of the remaining Directors, though less than a quorum. Each person so elected shall serve until the duration of the unexpired term, or until the next annual meeting.

11. Removal. Any Director may be removed by majority vote of the remaining Directors with or without cause.

12. Compensation. Directors shall receive no compensation for their service as Directors.

ARTICLE V
Officers

1. Designation of Officers. The Officers of the Corporation shall be the President, Vice President, Secretary, and Treasurer, and they shall have authority to carry out the duties prescribed in these Bylaws. The initial Officers of the Corporation shall be elected by the Board of Directors and shall serve for one year. One person may hold more than one office, but no person may hold the offices of both President and Secretary.[94]

2. Officers shall be current residents, property owners, business operators, or employees of the town.

3. Election and Term. Officers of the Corporation shall be reelected at the annual meeting of the Board of Directors and shall serve for one year, or until their replacements are elected and qualified.

4. Removal. At any regular or special meeting, any Officer may be removed by majority vote of the Board of Directors with or without cause.

5. Compensation. Officers of the Corporation shall receive no compensation for their service as Officers.

---

94 This may depend on your particular state law.

6. Vacancy. Vacancies, in any office for any reason, shall be filled by the Board of Directors for the unexpired term of office.

7. Board Service. Officers of the Corporation may also serve on the Board of Directors.

8. Duties of Officers.

    (a) President: The President is the Chief Executive Officer of this Corporation and will, subject to the control of the Board of Directors or any Committees, supervise and control the affairs of the Corporation. The President will perform all duties incident to the office of President and any other duties that may be required by these Bylaws or prescribed by the Board of Directors.

    (b) Vice President: The Vice President will perform all duties and exercise all powers of the President when the President is absent or is otherwise unable to act. The Vice President will perform any other duties that may be prescribed by the Board of Directors.

    (c) Secretary: The Secretary will keep minutes of all meetings of the Board of Directors, be the custodian of the corporate records, give all notices as are required by law or by these Bylaws, and generally perform all duties incident to the office of Secretary and any other duties as may be required by law, by the Bylaws, or which may be assigned by the Board of Directors.

    (d) Treasurer: The Treasurer will have charge and custody of all funds of this Corporation and will deposit the funds as required by the Board of Directors, keep and maintain adequate and correct accounts of the Corporation's properties and business transactions, and render reports and accountings to the Directors. The Treasurer shall prepare and, upon approval of the board, submit all mandatory financial disclosures, such as IRS Form 990. The Treasurer will perform all duties incident to the office of Treasurer and any other duties that may be required by these Bylaws or prescribed by the Board of Directors.

ARTICLE VI
Restrictions on Actions

1. All the assets and earnings of the Corporation shall be used exclusively for its exempt purposes, including the payment of expenses incidental thereto. No part of any net earnings shall inure to the benefit of any employee of the Corporation or be distributed to its Directors, Officers, or any private person, except that the Corporation shall be empowered to pay reasonable compensation for services rendered and make payments and distributions in furtherance of the purposes set forth in Article II of these Bylaws.

2. Notwithstanding any other provision of these Bylaws, the Corporation will not carry on any activities not permitted by an organization exempt under Section 501(c)(3) of the Code, or the corresponding provision of any future federal law, or organizations whose contributions which are exempt under Section 170(c)(2) of the Code, or the corresponding provision of any future federal law. The Corporation shall have no capital stock, pay no dividends, distribute no part of its net income or assets to any Directors, Officers, and private property of the subscribers, Directors or Officers shall not be liable for the debts of the Corporation.

3. No substantial part of the Corporation's activity shall be for the carrying on of a campaign of propaganda or otherwise attempting to influence legislation. The Corporation shall not participate in any political campaign and will not engage in political campaigns or attempt to influence legislation or interfere with any political campaign on behalf of or in opposition to any candidate for public office.

ARTICLE VII
Contracts, Checks, Deposits, and Funds

1. Contracts. The President and the Treasurer may enter into any contract on behalf of the Corporation. The Board of Directors may authorize, by general resolution, a Director or Directors, an agent or

agents, in addition to persons authorized by these Bylaws, to enter into any contract on behalf of the Corporation.

2. Checks, Drafts, and Orders of Payment. All checks, drafts, notes, orders of payment, or other evidence of indebtedness issued in the name of the Corporation shall be signed by the President or the Treasurer or by an Officer or Board agent such as the Board of Directors may, from time to time, designate by general resolution of the Board of Directors.

3. Deposits. All funds of the Corporation shall be deposited from time to time to the credit of the Corporation in such banks, trust companies, or other depositories as the Board of Directors may designate.

4. Gifts. The Directors, collectively or individually, any Officer or designated agent may accept gifts, contributions, bequests, or devise of any property on behalf of the Corporation.

5. Loans. No Director, Officer or agent shall have the authority, on behalf of the Corporation, to enter into a loan or any other contract of indebtedness except by unanimous vote in a specific resolution of the Board of Directors. The authority designated by this provision shall be limited to a single and specific instance.

ARTICLE VIII

Organization of Volunteers[95]

1. Volunteers must be current residents, property owners, business operators, or employees of the town.

2. Normal (Non-emergency) Structure.

   a. The Corporation will establish Sections and Teams around the functional areas comprising the core activities necessary to its goals. Volunteers with expertise or interest in a functional area will be recruited to serve in these Sections and Teams.

---

95 Many attorneys may recommend that this section be included in a Board Manual instead of in the bylaws. A Board Manual can be easily updated any time a committee is created, dissolved or restructured, whereas bylaws have to be amended. I am including this provision here as it illustrates the structure of the organization and has a good deal of initial guidance for a new organization. Also, this is the higher level part of the structure and less likely to be significantly changed.

b. The following initial four Sections will be established. Teams will be established as resources permit:
    i.   Planning Section
    ii. Operations Section
         A. Medical Team
         B. Security Team (militia)
         C. Communications Team
         D. Safety, Health, and Sanitation Team
         E. Legal Team (court)
    iii. Logistics Section
         A. Food Team
         B. Water Team
         C. Alternative Power, Equipment, and Skills Team
    iv. Finance and Community Outreach Section
c. Additional Sections and Teams may be established, or Sections and Teams may be merged, reorganized, or abolished by the Board of Directors. ICS Principles of organization and "span of control" should be considered in structural decisions.
d. The President will appoint one Volunteer as the "Section Chief" of each Section. A Volunteer may serve in more than one Section but may only serve as the Section Chief of one Section at one time.
e. Section Chiefs will be appointed for a term of two years.
f. The President and Section Chief may create further leadership positions (such as Team Leaders) in Sections and Teams, as deemed necessary for efficient operation.
g. A Director, Officer, or Volunteer may serve as a Section Chief or in a leadership position within the Sections or Teams.
h. Plans, outreach products, and other deliverables developed by the Sections must be approved by the President and submitted to the Board of Directors for review. The Board of Directors may amend or edit plans and products by a majority vote.
i. The Board of Directors may establish special qualification requirements for certain positions, as it deems necessary.

3. Emergency Structure (upon activation of Civil Defense):

    a. In an emergency in which the town requests assistance from the Corporation, the President (or Acting President) may authorize the Section Chiefs and Team Leaders to coordinate emergency efforts directly with the appropriate official(s) of the town government for the duration of the emergency.

    b. The Board of Directors will establish and distribute to all Directors, Officers, and Section Chiefs a written succession plan for an "Acting President" in the event that the President and Vice President are unavailable in an emergency.

    c. An Officer or Director will normally deploy to the town hall (or other designated command post) in an emergency to assist in coordinating overall efforts and resources available from the Corporation.

ARTICLE IX
Limitation on Liability

[It is critical that a provision indemnifying Directors and Officers be included. This will be a state specific provision which will need to comply with the applicable state law.]

ARTICLE X
Dissolution[96]

1. Upon dissolution of the Corporation, the Board of Directors shall, after paying or making provision for payment of all liabilities of the Corporation, including the costs and expenses of such dissolution, distribute all assets for one or more exempt purposes within the meaning of section 501(c)(3) of the Internal Revenue Code, or the corresponding section of any future federal tax code, or shall be distributed to the federal government, or to a state or local government, for a

---

96 Often the bylaws will specify the vote required for dissolution and often it will be a supermajority. The state statute will provide a default if it is not stated.

public purpose. Any such assets not so disposed of shall be disposed of by a court of competent Jurisdiction of the county in which the principal office of the Corporation is then located, exclusively for such purposes or to such organization or organizations, as said Court shall determine, which are organized and operated exclusively for such purposes.

ARTICLE XI
Statement of Nondiscrimination

1. Notwithstanding any provision of these Bylaws, the Corporation shall not discriminate against any director, officer, employee, applicant, volunteer, or participant on the basis of sex, race, color, ethnicity, or national origin.

ARTICLE XII
Compliance Code

1. The Board of Directors shall adopt and maintain a Compliance Code which will be applicable to all Directors, Officers, Employees and Volunteers of the Corporation. Such code will consist of the following policies:
    a. Code of Ethics
    b. Conflict of Interest Policy
    c. Whistleblower Protection Policy
    d. Document Retention and Destruction Policy
    e. Any other compliance policies required by law

ARTICLE XIII
Amendments to Bylaws and Articles of Incorporation

1. The Board of Directors shall have the power to amend, alter, make, and repeal the Bylaws and Articles of Incorporation of the Corporation by majority vote.

Adoption of Bylaws

Adopted by the Board of Directors by resolution and vote of all directors on the date below:

____ [Signature/Date]
[First Board Member's Name Here]

____ [Signature/Date]
[Second Board Member's Name Here]

____ [Signature/Date]
[Third Board Member's Name Here]

Bylaws (Sample #2: With Members)[97]

BYLAWS OF [Town Y] Civil Defense Corp.

ARTICLE I
Name, Office, and Duration

1. Name. The name of the Corporation is [Town Y] Civil Defense Corp.
2. Location. The principle place of business and administrative office shall be located at [address].
3. Duration. The Corporation shall have perpetual existence.

ARTICLE II
Purpose

1. The nature of the activities to be conducted or the purposes of the Corporation are to engage in any lawful act or activity permitted under the Nonprofit Corporation Law of [State], (the "Act") which is charitable, religious, educational and/or scientific in nature, entitling the Corporation to exemption from taxation under Section 501(c)(3) of the Internal Revenue Code of 1986, as the same may be amended and in force from time to time (the "Code"), and more particularly:
   (a) To educate and promote individual, family, and town preparedness for disasters;
   (b) To provide disaster assistance and relief to town residents in the event of a disaster; and
   (c) To educate and provide planning and resource options to the town for preparation and response to a "worst-case," long-term catastrophe affecting the town.

---

97 Many attorneys may advise *against* structuring a nonprofit organization with members unless required by the state, or in the case of organizations that will have dues-paying members. This example is an organization with dues-paying members.

ARTICLE III
Membership

1. Eligibility for membership: Application for voting membership shall be open to any current resident, property owner, business operator, or employee of the town that supports the purpose statement in Article II. Membership is granted after completion and receipt of a membership application and annual dues. All memberships shall be granted upon a majority vote of the Board.

2. Annual dues: The amount required for annual dues shall be $100 each year, unless changed by a majority vote of the members at an annual meeting of the full membership. Continued membership is contingent upon being up-to-date on membership dues.

3. Rights of members: Each member shall be eligible to vote or appoint by written proxy one voting representative to cast the member's vote in elections.

4. Resignation and termination: Any member may resign by filing a written resignation with the secretary. Resignation shall not relieve a member of unpaid dues or other charges previously accrued. A member can have his or her membership terminated by a majority vote of the Board, with or without cause.

5. Volunteers: Any current resident, property owner, business operator, or employee of the town that supports the purpose statement in Article II may volunteer for Civil Defense activities. Volunteers who are not members are not eligible to vote in elections.

ARTICLE IV
Meetings of Members

1. Regular meetings: Regular meetings of the members shall be held quarterly, at a time and place designated by the President.

2. Annual meetings: An annual meeting of the members shall take place in the month of October, the specific date, time and location of which will be designated by the President. At the annual meeting, the

members shall elect directors, receive reports on the activities of the association, and determine the amount of the annual dues of members for the coming year.

3. Special meetings: Special meetings may be called by the President or a simple majority of the Board of Directors. A petition signed by 5 percent of voting members may also call a special meeting.

4. Notice of meetings: Written notice of each annual or special meeting shall be sent to each voting member not less than two weeks prior to the meeting.

5. Quorum: The members present at any properly announced meeting shall constitute a quorum.

6. Voting: All issues to be voted on shall be decided by a simple majority of those present at the meeting in which the vote takes place.

ARTICLE V
Board of Directors

1. Election and Term of Office.[98] The members of the initial Board of Directors of the Corporation shall be those individuals named in the Articles of Incorporation and shall serve until their successors are elected. The Board of Directors shall serve terms of three years.

2. Number. The initial number of Directors shall be three (3) and may be increased or decreased without further amendment of these Bylaws. At no time may the number of Directors be less than three (3).

3. Qualifications. To serve as a Director, an individual shall be a resident, property owner, business operator, or employee of the town and shall have one of or any combination of the following qualifications:
   (a) Prior experience serving on a nonprofit board
   (b) Law enforcement training and experience
   (c) Military training and experience

---

98 The initial Directors should be elected as part of the incorporation process, either in the certificate of incorporation or in a "consent" signed by the incorporator(s). An alternative to 1 year terms would be staggered or classified terms. A common method is 3 year staggered terms, with the possibility that 1/3 of the Board rotates off in any given year.

(d) Fire, EMS or Emergency Management training and experience

(e) Medical training and experience

(f) General business or entrepreneurial experience

(g) Training and experience in specific skill sets sought by the Board and shall have a desire to use his or her knowledge, skills, and resources to help the town to survive and recover from worst-case disaster scenarios.

4. Powers. The Board of Directors shall have all corporate authority, except such powers as are otherwise provided in these Bylaws and the laws of the State of ________, to conduct the affairs of the Corporation in accordance with these Bylaws. The Board of Directors may, by general resolution, delegate to committees of their own number, or to Officers of the Corporation, such powers as they deem appropriate.

5. Regular Board Meetings. Regular meetings of the Board of Directors shall be held at the place and time designated by the Board of Directors including phone conference calls, and monthly or annual meetings, or otherwise called by a majority of the Board of Directors.

6. Special Meetings. Special meetings may be called by the President of the Corporation or a majority of the Board of Directors. Persons authorized to call special meetings shall provide written notice of the time and location of such meetings and state the purpose thereof, and no other matter shall be considered by the Board of Directors at such special meeting except upon unanimous vote of all Directors present. At least two days advance notice is required for special meetings.

7. Annual Board Meetings. Directors may meet each year for the purpose of organization and transaction of other business. The time and location of such meeting shall be noticed in writing.

8. Notice and Waiver. Notice of regular meetings need not be in writing. Attendance at any meeting shall be considered waiver of the notice requirement thereof.

9. Quorum. A majority of the Directors then in office shall constitute a quorum for the transaction of business at any meeting of the Board of Directors. A majority vote of a quorum present at a meeting is

required for any action by the Board. Any amendment to the Bylaws requires a majority vote all directors then in office.

10. Vacancy. Any vacancy occurring in the Board of Directors shall be filled by majority vote of the remaining Directors, though less than a quorum. Each person so selected shall serve until the next annual meeting.

11. Nominations.

    a. The Board's Nominating Committee shall submit its nominations and bios for Directors to the Secretary in time for distribution with the annual meeting notice to members.

    b. A petition signed by 10 percent of voting members may also submit nominations and bios to the Secretary provided that it is received in time for distribution with the annual meeting notice to members, and that said nominees meet the qualifications for Director.

12. Removal. Any Director may be removed by majority vote of the remaining Directors, with our without cause.

13. Compensation. Directors shall receive no compensation for their service as Directors.

ARTICLE VI
Officers

1. Designation of Officers. The officers of the Corporation shall be the President, Vice President, Secretary, and Treasurer, and they shall have authority to carry out the duties prescribed in these Bylaws. The initial Officers of the Corporation shall be elected by the Board of Directors and shall serve for one year. One person may hold more than one office, but no person may hold the offices of both President and Secretary.[99]

---

99 This may depend on your particular state law.

2. Officers shall be residents, property owners, business operators, or employees of the town.

3. Election and Term. Officers of the Corporation shall be reelected at the annual meeting of the Board of Directors and shall serve for one year, or until their replacements are elected and qualified.

4. Removal. At any regular or special meeting, any officer may be removed by majority vote of the Board of Directors with or without cause.

5. Compensation. Officers of the Corporation shall receive no compensation for their service as officers.

6. Vacancy. Vacancies, in any office for any reason, shall be filled by the Board of Directors for the unexpired term of office.

7. Board Service. Officers of the Corporation may also serve on the Board of Directors.

8. Duties of Officers.

   (a) President: The President is the Chief Executive Officer of this Corporation and will, subject to the control of the Board of Directors or any Committees, supervise and control the affairs of the Corporation. The President will perform all duties incident to the office of President and any other duties that may be required by these Bylaws or prescribed by the Board of Directors. The President will preside over the meetings of the members.

   (b) Vice President: The Vice President will perform all duties and exercise all powers of the President when the President is absent or is otherwise unable to act. The Vice President will perform any other duties that may be prescribed by the Board of Directors.

   (c) Secretary: The Secretary will keep minutes of all meetings of the members and Board of Directors, be the custodian of the corporate records, give all notices as are required by law or by these Bylaws, and generally perform all duties incident to the office of Secretary and any other duties as may be required by law, by the Bylaws, or which may be assigned by the Board of Directors.

(d) Treasurer: The Treasurer will have charge and custody of all funds of this Corporation, and will deposit the funds as required by the Board of Directors, keep and maintain adequate and correct accounts of the Corporation's properties and business transactions, and render reports and accountings to the Directors. The Treasurer shall prepare and, upon approval of the Board, submit all mandatory financial disclosures, such as IRS Form 990. The Treasurer will perform all duties incident to the office of Treasurer and any other duties that may be required by these Bylaws or prescribed by the Board of Directors.

ARTICLE VII
Restrictions on Actions

1. All the assets and earnings of the Corporation shall be used exclusively for its exempt purposes, including the payment of expenses incidental thereto. No part of any net earnings shall inure to the benefit of any employee of the Corporation or be distributed to its Directors, Officers, or any private person, except that the Corporation shall be empowered to pay reasonable compensation for services rendered and make payments and distributions in furtherance of the purposes set forth in Article II of these Bylaws.

2. Notwithstanding any other provision of these Bylaws, the Corporation will not carry on any activities not permitted by an organization exempt under Section 501(c)(3) of the Code, or the corresponding provision of any future federal law, or organizations whose contributions which are exempt under Section 170(c)(2) of the Code, or the corresponding provision of any future federal law. The Corporation shall have no capital stock, pay no dividends, distribute no part of its net income or assets to any Directors, Officers, and private property of the subscribers, Directors, or Officers shall not be liable for the debts of the Corporation.

3. No substantial part of the Corporation's activity shall be for the carrying on of a campaign of propaganda or otherwise attempting to influence legislation. The Corporation shall not participate in any political campaign and will not engage in political campaigns or attempt to influence legislation or interfere with any political campaign on behalf or in opposition to any candidate for public office.

ARTICLE VIII
Contracts, Checks, Deposits, and Funds

1. Contracts. The President or the Treasurer may enter into any contract on behalf of the Corporation. The Board of Directors may authorize, by general resolution, a Director or Directors, an agent or agents, in addition to persons authorized by these Bylaws to enter into any contract on behalf of the Corporation.
2. Checks, Drafts, and Orders of Payment. All checks, drafts, notes, orders of payment, or other evidence of indebtedness issued in the name of the Corporation shall be signed by the President or the Treasurer or by an Officer or Board agent such as the Board of Directors may, from time to time, designate by general resolution of the Board of Directors.
3. Deposits. All funds of the Corporation shall be deposited from time to time to the credit of the Corporation in such banks, trust companies, or other depositories as the Board of Directors may designate.
4. Gifts. The Directors, collectively or individually, any Officer or designated agent may accept gifts, contributions, bequests, or devise of any property on behalf of the Corporation.
5. Loans. No Director, Officer, or agent shall have the authority, on behalf of the Corporation, to enter into a loan or any other contract of indebtedness except by unanimous vote in a specific resolution of

the Board of Directors. The authority designated by this provision shall be limited to a single and specific instance.

ARTICLE IX
Organization of Members and Volunteers[100]

1. Volunteers shall be residents, property owners, business operators, or employees of the town.
2. Normal (Non-emergency) Structure.
   a. The Corporation will establish Sections and Teams around the functional areas comprising the core activities necessary to its goals. Members and Volunteers with expertise or interest in a functional area will be recruited to serve in these Sections and Teams.
   b. The following initial four Sections will be established. Teams will be established as resources permit:
      i. Planning Section
      ii. Operations Section
         A. Medical Team
         B. Security Team (militia)
         C. Communications Team
         D. Safety, Health, and Sanitation Team
         E. Legal Team (court)
      iii. Logistics Section
         A. Food Team
         B. Water Team
         C. Alternative Power, Equipment, and Skills Team
      iv. Finance and Community Outreach Section

---

100 Many attorneys may recommend that this section be included in a Board Manual instead of in the Bylaws. A Board Manual can be easily updated any time a committee is created, dissolved or restructured, whereas bylaws have to be amended. I am including this provision here as it illustrates the structure of the organization and has a good deal of initial guidance for a new organization. Also, this is the higher level part of the structure and less likely to be significantly changed.

c. Additional Sections and Teams may be established, or Sections and Teams may be merged, reorganized, or abolished by the Board of Directors. ICS Principles of organization and "span of control" should be considered in structural decisions.

d. The President will appoint one Volunteer as the "Section Chief" of each Section. A Volunteer may serve in more than one Section but may only serve as the Section Chief of one Section at one time.

e. Section Chiefs will be appointed for a term of two years.

f. The President and Section Chief may create further leadership positions (such as Team Leaders) in Sections and Teams, as deemed necessary for efficient operation.

g. A Director, Officer, Member, or Volunteer may serve as a Section Chief or in a leadership position within the Sections or Teams.

h. Plans, outreach products, and other deliverables developed by the Sections must be approved by the President and submitted to the Board of Directors for review. The Board of Directors may amend or edit plans and products by a majority vote.

i. The Board of Directors may establish special qualification requirements for certain positions, as it deems necessary.

3. Emergency Structure (upon activation of Civil Defense):

a. In an emergency in which the town requests assistance from the Corporation, the President (or Acting President) may authorize the Section Chiefs and Team Leaders to coordinate emergency efforts directly with the appropriate official(s) of the town government for the duration of the emergency.

b. The Board of Directors will establish and distribute to all Directors, Officers, and Section Chiefs a written succession plan for an "Acting President" in the event that the President and Vice President are unavailable in an emergency.

c. An Officer or Director will normally deploy to the town hall (or other designated command post) in an emergency to assist in coordinating overall efforts and resources available from the Corporation.

ARTICLE X
Limitation on Liability

[It is critical that a provision indemnifying Directors and Officers be included. This will be a state specific provision which will need to comply with the applicable state law.]

ARTICLE XI
Dissolution[101]

1. Upon dissolution of the Corporation, the Board of Directors shall, after paying or making provision for payment of all liabilities of the Corporation, including the costs and expenses of such dissolution, distribute all assets for one or more exempt purposes within the meaning of section 501(c)(3) of the Internal Revenue Code, or the corresponding section of any future federal tax code, or shall be distributed to the federal government, or to a state or local government, for a public purpose. Any such assets not so disposed of shall be disposed of by a court of competent Jurisdiction of the county in which the principal office of the Corporation is then located, exclusively for such purposes or to such organization or organizations, as said Court shall determine, which are organized and operated exclusively for such purposes.

ARTICLE XII
Statement of Nondiscrimination

1. Notwithstanding any provision of these Bylaws, the Corporation shall not discriminate against any Director, Officer, Employee, Applicant, Member, Volunteer, or Participant on the basis of sex, race, color, ethnicity, or national origin.

---

101 Often the bylaws will specify the vote required for dissolution and often it will be a supermajority. The state statute will provide a default if it is not stated.

ARTICLE XIII
Compliance Code

2. The Board of Directors shall adopt and maintain a Compliance Code, which will be applicable to all Directors, Officers, Employees, and Volunteers of the Corporation. Such code will consist of the following policies:
   f. Code of Ethics
   g. Conflict of Interest Policy
   h. Whistleblower Protection Policy
   i. Document Retention and Destruction Policy
   j. Any other compliance policies required by law

ARTICLE XIV
Amendments to Bylaws and Articles of Incorporation

1. The Board of Directors shall have the power to amend, alter, make, and repeal the Bylaws and Articles of Incorporation of the Corporation by majority vote.

Adoption of Bylaws

Adopted by the Board of Directors by resolution and vote of all directors on the date below:

_______________________________________ [Signature/Date]
[First Board Member's Name Here]

_______________________________________ [Signature/Date]
[Second Board Member's Name Here]

_______________________________________ [Signature/Date]
[Third Board Member's Name Here]

Appendix 3: Tabletop Exercises

While none of these exercises are directly on point, they may help you get started in developing a tabletop exercise for your community. The critical difference between most of the exercises below and "reality" is that no outside resources will be available. (In most of the following examples, the "apocalypse" is regional, so help is on the way from outside of the affected area.)

- *Long-Term Power Outage Preparedness (LTPO) in Wisconsin.* Wisconsin Department of Military Affairs, Division of Emergency Management. http://emergencymanagement.wi.gov/training/ltpo.asp (accessed August 6, 2017).
- *Power failure over a broad area of the United States.* U.S. Department of Homeland Security, FEMA. https://training.fema.gov/emiweb/is/is701a/visuals/05_is701a_macs_16feb2010.ppt (accessed August 6, 2017).
- *The Whole Community: Planning for the Unthinkable.* U.S. Department of Homeland Security, FEMA. https://www.fema.gov/media-library/assets/documents/26762 (accessed August 6, 2017).

There is a book by Chuck Manto that has EMP/GMD specific exercises: Manto, Charles. *Triple Threat Power Grid Exercise: High Impact Threats Workshop and Tabletop Exercises Examining Extreme Space Weather, EMP and Cyber Attacks.* Westphalia Press (October 30, 2015). ISBN-13: 978-1633912496.

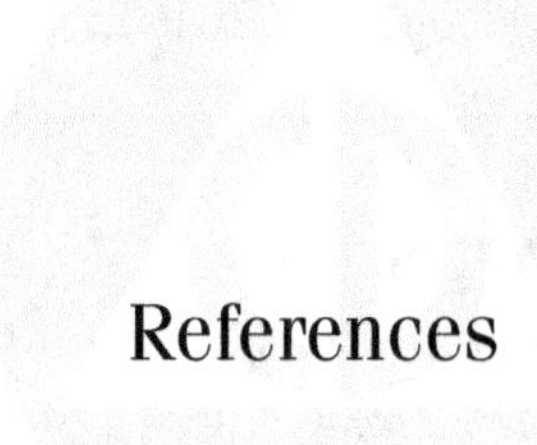

References

Federal Community Preparedness Pages:

Zombie Preparedness. U.S. Centers for Disease Control (CDC).
> https://www.cdc.gov/phpr/zombies.htm (accessed August 6, 2017).[102]

"Community Preparedness Toolkit." *Federal Emergency Management Agency (FEMA).*
> https://www.ready.gov/community-preparedness-toolkit (accessed August 6, 2017).

Laws Related to Power Grid Threats:

Public Law No: 114-92: National Defense Authorization Act for Fiscal Year 2016. November 25, 2015.
> https://www.congress.gov/114/plaws/publ92/PLAW-114publ92.pdf (accessed August 4, 2017).[103]

Public Law No. 114-328: National Defense Authorization Act for Fiscal Year 2017. December 23, 2016.

---

102 Honestly, this is my favorite government website!

103 See Section 1089. Reestablishment of Commission to Assess the Threat to the United States from Electromagnetic Pulse Attack.

https://www.gpo.gov/fdsys/pkg/PLAW-114publ328/pdf/PLAW-114publ328.pdf (accessed August 4, 2017).[104]

EMP Commission Reports:

"Executive Report." *Commission to Assess the Threat to the United States from Electromagnetic Pulse (EMP) Attack.* (2004).
http://www.empcommission.org/docs/empc_exec_rpt.pdf (accessed August 6, 2017).

"Critical National Infrastructures." *Commission to Assess the Threat to the United States from Electromagnetic Pulse (EMP) Attack.* (2008).
http://www.empcommission.org/docs/A2473-EMP_Commission-7MB.pdf (accessed August 6, 2017).

Reports from Federal Agencies and Commissions on Grid Security:

The Report of the President's Commission on Critical Infrastructure Protection. October 1997.
http://www.fas.org/sgp/library/pccip.pdf (accessed August 4, 2017).

U.S. General Accounting Office. *"Critical Infrastructure Protection" Testimony before the Subcommittee on Technology, Terrorism and Government Information, Committee on the Judiciary, U.S. Senate.* July 25, 2001.
https://www.gpo.gov/fdsys/pkg/GAOREPORTS-GAO-01-1005T/pdf/GAOREPORTS-GAO-01-1005T.pdf (accessed August 5, 2017).

---

104 See section 1913. EMP and GMD Planning, Research and Development, and Protection and Preparedness. Codified at 6 U.S.C. § 195f. EMP and GMD mitigation research and development. https://www.gpo.gov/fdsys/pkg/USCODE-2016-title6/pdf/USCODE-2016-title6-chap1-subchapIII-sec195f.pdf (accessed August 4, 2017).

U.S. General Accounting Office. *"Critical Infrastructure Protection" Report to the Committee on Governmental Affairs, U.S. Senate.* July 2002. http://www.gao.gov/new.items/d02474.pdf (accessed August 5, 2017).

U.S. General Accounting Office. *"Critical Infrastructure Protection" Testimony before the Subcommittee on Oversight and Investigations, Committee on Energy and Commerce, House of Representatives.* July 9, 2002. http://www.gao.gov/assets/110/109467.pdf (accessed August 5, 2017).

U. S. Government Accountability Office. *"Critical Infrastructure Protection" Challenges for Selected Agencies and Industry Sectors.* GAO-03-233, February 2003. https://www.gpo.gov/fdsys/pkg/GAOREPORTS-GAO-03-233/pdf/GAOREPORTS-GAO-03-233.pdf (accessed August 4, 2017).

National Academy of Sciences. *Severe Space Weather Events—Understanding Societal and Economic Impacts.* Washington: National Academies Press, 2008. https://download.nap.edu/catalog.php?record_id=12507 (accessed August 6, 2017).

Wilson, Clay. *High Altitude Electromagnetic Pulse (HEMP) and High Power Microwave (HPM) Devices: Threat Assessments.* Washington: Congressional Research Service, July 21, 2008. http://www.fas.org/sgp/crs/natsec/RL32544.pdf (accessed August 6, 2017).

Perry, William J., Chairman. *America's Strategic Posture. The Final Report of the Congressional Commission on the Strategic Posture of the United States.* Washington, 2009. https://www.usip.org/sites/default/files/America's_Strategic_Posture_Auth_Ed.pdf (accessed August 5, 2017).

Oak Ridge National Laboratory. *Electromagnetic Pulse: Effects on the U.S. Power Grid.* Oak Ridge, TN: January, 2010. https://www.ferc.gov/industries/electric/indus-act/reliability/cybersecurity/ferc_meta-r-320.pdf (accessed August 6, 2017).

Executive Summary. https://www.ferc.gov/industries/electric/indus-act/reliability/cybersecurity/ferc_executive_summary.pdf (accessed August 6, 2017).

High-Impact, Low-Frequency Event Risk to the North American Bulk Power System. NERC / DOE. Washington, June 2010. https://energy.gov/sites/prod/files/High-Impact%20Low-Frequency%20Event%20Risk%20to%20the%20North%20American%20Bulk%20Power%20System%20-%202010.pdf (accessed August 5, 2017).

Oreskovic, Robert S. (Colonel) U.S. Army War College. *Electromagnetic Pulse—A Catastrophic Threat to the Homeland.* March, 24, 2011. http://www.hsdl.org/?view&did=724415 (accessed August 5, 2017).

National Academy of Sciences. *Terrorism and the Electric Power Delivery System.* Washington: National Academies Press, 2012. https://www.nap.edu/catalog/12050/terrorism-and-the-electric-power-delivery-system (accessed August 5, 2017).

Testimony of Dr. Peter Vincent Pry, Executive Director Task Force On National and Homeland Security, before the U.S. Federal Energy Regulatory Commission Technical Conference on Geomagnetic Disturbances to the Bulk Power System. April 30, 2012. https://www.ferc.gov/CalendarFiles/20120502132652-Pry,%20Homeland%20Security.pdf (accessed August 5, 2017).

Fischer, Eric A. *Federal Laws Relating to Cybersecurity: Overview and Discussion of Proposed Revisions.* Congressional Research Service. Washington, June 20, 2013. https://fas.org/sgp/crs/natsec/R42114.pdf (accessed August 5, 2017).

Interagency Security Committee. *Presidential Policy Directive 21 Implementation: An Interagency Security Committee White Paper.* February 2015. https://www.dhs.gov/sites/default/files/publications/ISC-PPD-21-Implementation-White-Paper-2015-508.pdf (accessed August 4, 2017).

U. S. Government Accountability Office. *Critical Infrastructure Protection: Preliminary Observations on DHS Efforts to Address Electromagnetic Threats to the Electric Grid*, GAO-15-692T, July 22, 2015. http://www.gao.gov/assets/680/671554.pdf (accessed August 4, 2017).

U. S. Government Accountability Office. *Critical Infrastructure Protection: Federal Agencies Have Taken Actions to Address Electromagnetic Risks, but Opportunities Exist to Further Assess Risks and Strengthen Collaboration.* GAO-16-243, March 2016. https://www.gao.gov/assets/680/676030.pdf (accessed August 4, 2017).

U.S. Department of Homeland Security. *Electromagnetic Pulse (EMP) Protection and Restoration Guidelines for Equipment and Facilities.* December 22, 2016. https://www.empcenter.org/storage/DHS%20App%20A-C%20 EMP%20Protect%20Restore%20%20EquipFacilities%20Ver1.pdf (accessed August 4, 2017).

U.S. Department of Energy and Electric Power Research Institute. Joint Electromagnetic Pulse Resilience Strategy. July 2016. https://www.energy.gov/sites/prod/files/2016/07/f33/DOE_ EMPStrategy_July2016_0.pdf (accessed August 6, 2017).

U.S. Department of Energy Electromagnetic Pulse Resilience Action Plan. January 2017. https://energy.gov/sites/prod/files/2017/01/f34/DOE%20EMP%20 Resilience%20Action%20Plan%20January%202017.pdf (accessed August 6, 2017).

Executive Orders and Presidential Documents

Executive Order 13010: Critical Infrastructure Protection. July 15, 1996. http://www.gpo.gov/fdsys/pkg/FR-1996-07-17/pdf/96-18351.pdf (accessed August 4, 2017).

Executive Order 13064: Further Amendment to Executive Order 13010, as Amended, Critical Infrastructure Protection. October 11, 1997. http://www.gpo.gov/fdsys/pkg/FR-1997-10-16/pdf/97-27644.pdf (accessed August 4, 2017).

Presidential Decision Directive 63: Critical Infrastructure Protection. May 22, 1998. http://www.fas.org/irp/offdocs/pdd/pdd-63.pdf (accessed August 4, 2017).

Executive Order 13231: Critical Infrastructure Protection in the Information Age. October 16, 2001. http://www.gpo.gov/fdsys/pkg/WCPD-2001-10-22/pdf/WCPD-2001-10-22-Pg1485.pdf (accessed August 4, 2017).

Executive Order 13286: Amendment of Executive Orders, and Other Actions, in Connection With the Transfer of Certain Functions to the Secretary of Homeland Security. February 28, 2003. http://www.gpo.gov/fdsys/pkg/WCPD-2003-03-10/pdf/WCPD-2003-03-10-Pg268.pdf (accessed August 4, 2017).

Presidential Directive HSPD-7: Critical Infrastructure Identification, Prioritization and Protection. December 17, 2003. https://www.gpo.gov/fdsys/pkg/PPP-2003-book2/pdf/PPP-2003-book2-doc-pg1739.pdf (accessed August 4, 2017).

Executive Order 13636: Improving Critical Infrastructure Cybersecurity. February 12, 2013. http://www.gpo.gov/fdsys/pkg/FR-2013-02-19/pdf/2013-03915.pdf (accessed August 4, 2017).

Presidential Policy Directive 21 (PPD-21): Critical Infrastructure Security and Resilience. February 12, 2013. https://obamawhitehouse.archives.gov/the-press-office/2013/02/12/presidential-policy-directive-critical-infrastructure-security-and-resil (accessed August 4, 2017).

Congressional Hearings, Reports (and Failed Legislation) on Threats to the Grid:

Threat Posed By Electromagnetic Pulse (EMP) to US Military Systems and Civil Infrastructure, Before U.S. House Subcommittee on Military Research and Development of the Committee on National Security, 105th Congress (July 16, 1997). http://commdocs.house.gov/committees/security/has197010.000/ has197010_0.HTM (accessed August 6, 2017).

Electromagnetic Pulse (EMP): Should This Be a Problem of National Concern to Private Enterprise, Businesses Small and Large, As Well As Government? Before the U.S. House, Subcommittee on Government Programs and Oversight of the Committee on Small Business, 106th Congress (June 1, 1999). http://www.gpo.gov/fdsys/pkg/CHRG-106hhrg59747/pdf/CHRG-106hhrg59747.pdf (accessed August 6, 2017).

Implications of Power Blackouts for the Nation's Cybersecurity and Critical Infrastructure Protection, Before the U.S. House, Joint Hearing of the Subcommittee on Cybersecurity, Science, and Research and Development, and the Subcommittee on Infrastructure and Border Security of the Select Committee On Homeland Security, 108th Congress (September 2003). http://www.gpo.gov/fdsys/pkg/CHRG-108hhrg99793/pdf/CHRG-108hhrg99793.pdf (accessed August 6, 2017).

Blackout 2003: How Did It Happen and Why? Before the Committee on Energy and Commerce. (108th Congress) September 3, 2003. https://www.gpo.gov/fdsys/pkg/CHRG-108hhrg89467/pdf/CHRG-108hhrg89467.pdf (accessed August 5, 2017).

Keeping the Lights On: The Federal Role in Managing the Nation's Electricity. Before the Committee on Governmental Affairs, Oversight of Government Management, the Federal Workforce and the District of Columbia Subcommittee. (108th Congress) September 10, 2003.

https://www.gpo.gov/fdsys/pkg/CHRG-108shrg90232/pdf/CHRG-108shrg90232.pdf (accessed August 5, 2017).

Keeping the Lights On: Removing Barriers to Technology to Prevent Blackouts. Before the Committee on Energy. (108th Congress) September 25, 2003. https://www.gpo.gov/fdsys/pkg/CHRG-108hhrg89419/pdf/CHRG-108hhrg89419.pdf (accessed August 5, 2017).

What Is Space Weather and Who Should Forecast It? Before the U.S. House, Subcommittee on Environment, Technology, and Standards, Committee on Science, 108th Congress (October 30, 2003). http://www.gpo.gov/fdsys/pkg/CHRG-108hhrg90161/pdf/CHRG-108hhrg90161.pdf (accessed August 6, 2017).

The Report of the Commission to Assess the Threat to the U.S. from Electromagnetic Pulse Attack, Before the U.S. House Committee On Armed Services, 108th Congress (July 22, 2004). http://commdocs.house.gov/committees/security/has204000.000/has204000_0.HTM (accessed August 5, 2017) or https://www.loc.gov/resource/conghear09.0014772214A/?sp=1&st=single (accessed August 5, 2017).

Terrorism and the EMP Threat to Homeland Security, Before the U.S. Senate, Subcommittee on Terrorism, Technology and Homeland Security of the Committee on the Judiciary, 109th Congress (March 8, 2005). http://www.gpo.gov/fdsys/pkg/CHRG-109shrg21324/pdf/CHRG-109shrg21324.pdf (accessed August 6, 2017).

Cyber Security: U.S. Vulnerability and Preparedness, Before the U.S. House, Committee on Science, 109th Congress (September 15, 2005). http://www.gpo.gov/fdsys/pkg/CHRG-109hhrg23332/pdf/CHRG-109hhrg23332.pdf (accessed August 6, 2017).

The Cyber Threat to Control Systems: Stronger Regulations Are Necessary to Secure the Electric Grid. Before the Committee on Homeland Security, Subcommittee on Emerging Threats, Cybersecurity, and Science and Technology. (110th Congress) October 17, 2007. https://www.gpo.gov/fdsys/pkg/CHRG-110hhrg48973/pdf/CHRG-110hhrg48973.pdf (accessed August 5, 2017).

Implications of Cyber Vulnerabilities on the Resilience and Security of the Electric Grid. Before the Committee on Homeland Security, Subcommittee on Emerging Threats, Cybersecurity, and Science and Technology. (110th Congress) May 21, 2008. https://www.gpo.gov/fdsys/pkg/CHRG-110hhrg43177/pdf/CHRG-110hhrg43177.pdf (accessed August 5, 2017).

Threat Posed by Electromagnetic Pulse (EMP) Attack, Before the U.S. House, Committee on Armed Services, 110th Congress (July 10, 2008). http://www.gpo.gov/fdsys/pkg/CHRG-110hhrg45133/pdf/CHRG-110hhrg45133.pdf (accessed August 6, 2017).

Defeating the Improvised Explosive Device (IED) and Other Asymmetric Threats: Today's Efforts and Tomorrow's Requirements, Before the U.S. House, Oversight and Investigations Subcommittee of the Committee on Armed Services, 110th Congress (September 16, 2008). http://www.gpo.gov/fdsys/pkg/CHRG-110hhrg45681/pdf/CHRG-110hhrg45681.pdf (accessed August 6, 2017).

Securing the Modern Electric Grid from Physical and Cyber Attacks, Before the U.S. House, Subcommittee on Emerging Threats, Cybersecurity, and Science and Technology of the Committee on Homeland Security, 111th Congress (July 21, 2009). http://www.gpo.gov/fdsys/pkg/CHRG-111hhrg53425/pdf/CHRG-111hhrg53425.pdf (accessed August 6, 2017).

Protecting the Electric Grid: H.R. 2165, The "Bulk Power System Protection Act of 2009," and H.R. 2195, Before the U.S. House, Subcommittee on Energy and Environment of the Committee on Energy and Commerce, 111th Congress (October 27, 2009).
http://www.gpo.gov/fdsys/pkg/CHRG-111hhrg74848/pdf/CHRG-111hhrg74848.pdf (accessed August 6, 2017).

Resourcing the National Defense Strategy: Implications of Long Term Defense Budget Trends, Before the U.S. House, Committee on Armed Services, 111th Congress (November 18, 2009).
http://www.gpo.gov/fdsys/pkg/CHRG-111hhrg56863/pdf/CHRG-111hhrg56863.pdf (accessed August 6, 2017).

Grid Reliability and Infrastructure Defense Act. House Report 111-493. 111th Congress (May 25, 2010).
https://www.gpo.gov/fdsys/pkg/CRPT-111hrpt493/pdf/CRPT-111hrpt493.pdf (accessed August 6, 2017).

Government Preparedness and Response to a Terrorist Attack Using Weapons of Mass Destruction, U.S. Senate, Subcommittee on Terrorism, Technology and Homeland Security of the Committee on the Judiciary, 111th Congress (August 4, 2010).
http://www.gpo.gov/fdsys/pkg/CHRG-111shrg64769/pdf/CHRG-111shrg64769.pdf (accessed August 6, 2017).

Grid Reliability and Infrastructure Defense Act. Senate Report 111-331. 111th Congress (Sept. 27, 2010).
https://www.gpo.gov/fdsys/pkg/CRPT-111srpt331/pdf/CRPT-111srpt331.pdf (accessed August 5, 2017).

H.R. 668 Secure High-voltage Infrastructure for Electricity from Lethal Damage Act; SHIELD Act. 112th Congress (February 11, 2011).
https://www.gpo.gov/fdsys/pkg/BILLS-112hr668ih/pdf/BILLS-112hr668ih.pdf (accessed August 5, 2017).

Cyber Security, Before the U.S. Senate, Committee on Energy and Natural Resources, 112th Congress (May 5, 2011). http://www.gpo.gov/fdsys/pkg/CHRG-112shrg67362/pdf/CHRG-112shrg67362.pdf (accessed August 6, 2017).

Protecting the Electric Grid: H.R. ————, The Grid Reliability and Infrastructure Defense Act, Before the U.S. House, Subcommittee on Energy and Power of the Committee on Energy and Commerce, 112th Congress (May 31, 2011). http://www.gpo.gov/fdsys/pkg/CHRG-112hhrg72383/pdf/CHRG-112hhrg72383.pdf (accessed August 6, 2017).

Senate Report 112-34 Grid Cyber Security Act. 112th Congress (July 11, 2011). http://www.gpo.gov/fdsys/pkg/CRPT-112srpt34/pdf/CRPT-112srpt34.pdf (accessed August 5, 2017).

Update On KC-46A and Legacy Aerial Refueling Aircraft Programs, Before the U.S. House, Subcommittee on Seapower and Projection Forces of the Committee on Armed Services, 112th Congress (October 13, 2011). http://www.gpo.gov/fdsys/pkg/CHRG-112hhrg71448/pdf/CHRG-112hhrg71448.pdf (accessed August 6, 2017).

Electric Grid Security, Before the U.S. Senate, Committee on Energy and Natural Resources, 112th Congress (July 17, 2012). http://www.gpo.gov/fdsys/pkg/CHRG-112shrg75809/pdf/CHRG-112shrg75809.pdf (accessed August 6, 2017).

H. Res. 762: Expressing the sense of the House of Representatives regarding community-based civil defense and power generation. 112th Congress (August 2, 2012). http://www.gpo.gov/fdsys/pkg/BILLS-112hres762ih/pdf/BILLS-112hres762ih.pdf (accessed August 4, 2017).

The EMP Threat: Examining the Consequences. Hearing before the Homeland Security Committee, Subcommittee on Cybersecurity, Infrastructure Protection, and Security Technologies. Serial No. 112-115. 112th Congress (September 12, 2012).
http://www.gpo.gov/fdsys/pkg/CHRG-112hhrg80856/pdf/CHRG-112hhrg80856.pdf (accessed August 4, 2017).

Cyber Threats and Security Solutions, Before the U.S. House Committee on Energy and Commerce. 113th Congress (May 21, 2013).
https://www.gpo.gov/fdsys/pkg/CHRG-113hhrg82197/pdf/CHRG-113hhrg82197.pdf (accessed August 4, 2017).

Markey, Edward J. and Waxman, Henry A. *Electric Grid Vulnerability: Industry Responses Reveal Security Gaps.* U.S. House of Representatives. (May 21, 2013).
https://www.markey.senate.gov/imo/media/doc/Markey%20Grid%20Report_05.21.131.pdf (accessed August 4, 2017).

H.R. 2417 Secure High-voltage Infrastructure for Electricity from Lethal Damage (SHIELD Act). 113th Congress (June 18, 2013).
https://www.congress.gov/113/bills/hr2417/BILLS-113hr2417ih.pdf (accessed August 4, 2017).

House Report 113-102 National Defense Authorization Act. 113th Congress (June 7, 2013).
http://www.gpo.gov/fdsys/pkg/CRPT-113hrpt102/pdf/CRPT-113hrpt102.pdf (accessed August 4, 2017).

H.R. 3410 To amend the Homeland Security Act of 2002 to secure critical infrastructure against electromagnetic pulses, and for other purposes. 113th Congress (October 30, 2013). [This Act may be cited as the "Critical Infrastructure Protection Act" or "CIPA"].
http://www.gpo.gov/fdsys/pkg/BILLS-113hr3410ih/pdf/BILLS-113hr3410ih.pdf (accessed August 4, 2017).

Grid Reliability and Infrastructure Defense Act (GRID) Act. 113th Congress (March 26, 2014).
Senate Bill S. 2158: https://www.congress.gov/113/bills/s2158/BILLS-113s2158is.pdf (accessed August 4, 2017).
House Bill H.R. 4298: https://www.congress.gov/113/bills/hr4298/BILLS-113hr4298ih.pdf (accessed August 4, 2017).

S. Hrg. 114-483: Protecting the Electric Grid from the Potential Threats of Solar Storms and Electromagnetic Pulse. 114th Congress (July 22, 2015).
https://www.gpo.gov/fdsys/pkg/CHRG-114shrg22225/pdf/CHRG-114shrg22225.pdf (accessed August 4, 2017).

House Report 114-240: Critical Infrastructure Protection Act. 114th Congress (August 4, 2015).
https://www.congress.gov/114/crpt/hrpt240/CRPT-114hrpt240.pdf (accessed August 4, 2017).

H.R. 1073 Critical Infrastructure Protection Act. 114th Congress (November 16, 2015).
https://www.congress.gov/114/bills/hr1073/BILLS-114hr1073rfs.pdf (accessed August 4, 2017).

House Report 114-359 Providing for Further Consideration of the Bill (H.R. 8) to Modernize Energy Infrastructure. 114th Congress (December 1, 2015).
https://www.congress.gov/114/crpt/hrpt359/CRPT-114hrpt359.pdf (accessed August 4, 2017).

H.R. 8 North American Energy Security and Infrastructure Act of 2015. 114th Congress (December 2, 2015).
https://www.congress.gov/crec/2015/12/02/CREC-2015-12-02-pt1-PgH8894-2.pdf (accessed August 4, 2017).

H. Amdt. 842 to H.R.8 North American Energy Security and Infrastructure Act of 2015. 114th Congress (December 2, 2015).

https://www.congress.gov/crec/2015/12/02/CREC-2015-12-02-pt1-PgH8894-2.pdf (accessed August 4, 2017).

Senate Report 114-250: Critical Infrastructure Protection Act of 2015. 114th Congress (May 9, 2016).
https://www.congress.gov/114/crpt/srpt250/CRPT-114srpt250.pdf (accessed August 4, 2017).

Critical Infrastructure Protection Act of 2015, Report of the Committee on Homeland Security and Governmental Affairs, United States Senate to Accompany S. 1846, 114th Congress (May 9, 2016).
https://www.congress.gov/114/crpt/srpt250/CRPT-114srpt250.pdf (accessed August 4, 2017).

House Hearing: Oversight of Federal Efforts to Address Electromagnetic Risks. 114th Congress (May 17, 2016).
https://www.gpo.gov/fdsys/pkg/CHRG-114hhrg22762/pdf/CHRG-114hhrg22762.pdf (accessed August 4, 2017).

Assessing the Security of Critical Infrastructure: Threat, Vulnerabilities, and Solutions. Before the Committee on Homeland Security & Governmental Affairs. 114th Congress (May 18, 2016).
https://www.hsgac.senate.gov/hearings/assessing-the-security-of-critical-infrastructure-threat-vulnerabilities-and-solutions (accessed August 4, 2017).

House Hearing: Value of DHS's Vulnerability Assessments in Protecting our Nation's Critical Infrastructure. 114th Congress (July 12, 2016).
https://www.gpo.gov/fdsys/pkg/CHRG-114hhrg25264/pdf/CHRG-114hhrg25264.pdf (accessed August 4, 2017).

H.R. 945: Terrorism Prevention and Critical Infrastructure Protection Act of 2017. 115th Congress (February 7, 2017).

https://www.congress.gov/115/bills/hr945/BILLS-115hr945ih.pdf (accessed August 4, 2017).

Senate Report 115-12: Activities of the Committee on Homeland Security and Governmental Affairs. 115th Congress (March 28, 2017). https://www.gpo.gov/fdsys/pkg/CRPT-115srpt12/pdf/CRPT-115srpt12.pdf (accessed August 4, 2017).

House Hearing: Hearing to examine the threat posed by electromagnetic pulse and policy options to protect energy infrastructure and to improve capabilities for adequate system restoration. 115th Congress (May 4, 2017). https://www.energy.senate.gov/public/index.cfm/2017/5/hearing-to-examine-the-threat-posed-by-electromagnetic-pulse-and-policy-options-to-protect-energy-infrastructure-and-to-improve-capabilities-for-adequate-system-restoration (accessed August 4, 2017).

H.R. 2810: National Defense Authorization Act for Fiscal Year 2018. 115th Congress (July 18, 2017). https://www.gpo.gov/fdsys/pkg/BILLS-115hr2810pcs/pdf/BILLS-115hr2810pcs.pdf (accessed August 4, 2017). [See Section 1699B: "Commission to Assess the Threat to the United States from Electromagnetic Pulse Attacks and Events."]

Congressional Record on Electromagnetic Pulse Threats:

Congressional Record Volume 151 (June 9, 2005), pages H4340-4345. http://www.gpo.gov/fdsys/pkg/CREC-2005-06-09/pdf/CREC-2005-06-09-pt1-PgH4340.pdf (accessed August 6, 2017).

Congressional Record Volume 151 (June 21, 2005), pages H4888-4894. http://www.gpo.gov/fdsys/pkg/CREC-2005-06-21/pdf/CREC-2005-06-21-pt1-PgH4888-2.pdf (accessed August 6, 2017).

Congressional Record Volume 152 (September 7, 2006), pages H6352-6357. http://www.gpo.gov/fdsys/pkg/CREC-2006-09-07/pdf/CREC-2006-09-07-pt1-PgH6352.pdf (accessed August 6, 2017).

Congressional Record Volume 154 (July 10, 2008), pages H6393-6399. http://www.gpo.gov/fdsys/pkg/CREC-2008-07-10/pdf/CREC-2008-07-10-pt1-PgH6393.pdf (accessed August 6, 2017).

Congressional Record Volume 156 (March 25, 2010), pages H2446-2449. http://www.gpo.gov/fdsys/pkg/CREC-2010-03-25/pdf/CREC-2010-03-25-pt1-PgH2446-6.pdf (accessed August 6, 2017).

Congressional Record Volume 156 (July 20, 2010), pages H5760-5775. http://www.gpo.gov/fdsys/pkg/CREC-2010-07-20/pdf/CREC-2010-07-20-pt1-PgH5760.pdf (accessed August 6, 2017).

Congressional Record Volume 156 (November 30, 2010), pages H7743-7749. http://www.gpo.gov/fdsys/pkg/CREC-2010-11-30/pdf/CREC-2010-11-30-pt1-PgH7743-8.pdf (accessed August 6, 2017).

Congressional Record Volume 156 (December 1, 2010), page H7854, et seq. https://www.gpo.gov/fdsys/pkg/CREC-2010-12-01/pdf/CREC-2010-12-01-pt1-PgH7854-2.pdf (accessed August 6, 2017).

Congressional Record Volume 157 (February 11, 2011), page H7223, et seq. https://www.gpo.gov/fdsys/pkg/CREC-2011-02-11/pdf/CREC-2011-02-11-pt1-PgH722-2.pdf (accessed August 6, 2017).

Congressional Record Volume 157 (June 24, 2011), page H4573, et seq. https://www.gpo.gov/fdsys/pkg/CREC-2011-06-24/pdf/CREC-2011-06-24-pt1-PgH4573-2.pdf (accessed August 6, 2017).

Congressional Record Volume 157 (November 11, 2011), page S7998, et seq.

https://www.gpo.gov/fdsys/pkg/CREC-2011-11-29/pdf/CREC-2011-11-29-pt1-PgS7998-2.pdf (accessed August 6, 2017).

Congressional Record Volume 158 (May 17, 2012), page H2847, et seq. https://www.gpo.gov/fdsys/pkg/CREC-2012-05-17/pdf/CREC-2012-05-17-pt1-PgH2847.pdf (accessed August 6, 2017).

Congressional Record Volume 158 (July 19, 2012), page S5169, et seq. https://www.gpo.gov/fdsys/pkg/CREC-2012-07-19/pdf/CREC-2012-07-19-pt1-PgS5169-7.pdf (accessed August 6, 2017).

Congressional Record Volume 158 (July 30, 2012), page S5661, et seq. https://www.gpo.gov/fdsys/pkg/CREC-2012-07-30/pdf/CREC-2012-07-30-pt1-PgS5661.pdf (accessed August 6, 2017).

Congressional Record Volume 158 (August 2, 2012), page H5692, et seq. https://www.gpo.gov/fdsys/pkg/CREC-2012-08-02/pdf/CREC-2012-08-02-pt1-PgH5692.pdf (accessed August 6, 2017).

Congressional Record Volume 158 (December 19, 2012), page H7350-7353. http://www.gpo.gov/fdsys/pkg/CREC-2012-12-19/pdf/CREC-2012-12-19-pt1-PgH7350.pdf (accessed August 6, 2017).

Congressional Record Volume 159 (June 5, 2013), page H3162, et seq. https://www.gpo.gov/fdsys/pkg/CREC-2013-06-05/pdf/CREC-2013-06-05-pt1-PgH3162-4.pdf (accessed August 6, 2017).

Congressional Record Volume 159 (June 13, 2013), page H3382, et seq. https://www.gpo.gov/fdsys/pkg/CREC-2013-06-13/pdf/CREC-2013-06-13-pt1-PgH3382-2.pdf (accessed August 6, 2017).

Congressional Record Volume 159 (June 18, 2013), page H3758, et seq. https://www.gpo.gov/fdsys/pkg/CREC-2013-06-18/pdf/CREC-2013-06-18-pt1-PgH3758-2.pdf (accessed August 6, 2017).

Congressional Record Volume 159 (December 12, 2013), page H7894, et seq. https://www.gpo.gov/fdsys/pkg/CREC-2013-12-12/pdf/CREC-2013-12-12-pt1-PgH7894.pdf (accessed August 6, 2017).

Congressional Record Volume 160 (April 30, 2014), page H3358, et seq. https://www.gpo.gov/fdsys/pkg/CREC-2014-04-30/pdf/CREC-2014-04-30-pt1-PgH3358-5.pdf (accessed August 6, 2017).

Congressional Record Volume 160 (May 20, 2014), page H4541, et seq. https://www.gpo.gov/fdsys/pkg/CREC-2014-05-20/pdf/CREC-2014-05-20-pt1-PgH4541-2.pdf (accessed August 6, 2017).

Congressional Record Volume 160 (May 30, 2014), page H5034, et seq. https://www.gpo.gov/fdsys/pkg/CREC-2014-05-30/pdf/CREC-2014-05-30-pt1-PgH5034.pdf (accessed August 6, 2017).

Congressional Record Volume 160 (June 20, 2014), page H5563, et seq. https://www.gpo.gov/fdsys/pkg/CREC-2014-06-20/pdf/CREC-2014-06-20-pt1-PgH5563-3.pdf (accessed August 6, 2017).

Congressional Record Volume 160 (December 1, 2014), page H8194, et seq. https://www.gpo.gov/fdsys/pkg/CREC-2014-12-01/pdf/CREC-2014-12-01-pt1-PgH8194.pdf (accessed August 6, 2017).

Congressional Record Volume 160 (December 4, 2014), page H8671, et seq. https://www.gpo.gov/fdsys/pkg/CREC-2014-12-04/pdf/CREC-2014-12-04-pt2-PgH8671.pdf (accessed August 6, 2017).

Congressional Record Volume 160 (December 4, 2014), page H8385, et seq. https://www.gpo.gov/fdsys/pkg/CREC-2014-12-04/pdf/CREC-2014-12-04-pt1-PgH8385-4.pdf (accessed August 6, 2017).

Congressional Record Volume 160 (December 9, 2014), page S6464, et seq. https://www.gpo.gov/fdsys/pkg/CREC-2014-12-09/pdf/CREC-2014-12-09-pt1-PgS6464.pdf (accessed August 6, 2017).

Congressional Record Volume 160 (December 9, 2014), page S6450, et seq. https://www.gpo.gov/fdsys/pkg/CREC-2014-12-09/pdf/CREC-2014-12-09-pt1-PgS6450.pdf (accessed August 6, 2017).

Congressional Record Volume 160 (December 10, 2014), page H8951, et seq. https://www.gpo.gov/fdsys/pkg/CREC-2014-12-10/pdf/CREC-2014-12-10-pt1-PgH8951.pdf (accessed August 6, 2017).

Congressional Record Volume 161 (May 14, 2015), page H2999, et seq. https://www.gpo.gov/fdsys/pkg/CREC-2015-05-14/pdf/CREC-2015-05-14-pt1-PgH2999-3.pdf (accessed August 6, 2017).

Congressional Record Volume 161 (June 4, 2015), page S3784, et seq. https://www.gpo.gov/fdsys/pkg/CREC-2015-06-04/pdf/CREC-2015-06-04-pt1-PgS3784.pdf (accessed August 6, 2017).

Congressional Record Volume 161 (June 8, 2015), page S3866, et seq. https://www.gpo.gov/fdsys/pkg/CREC-2015-06-08/pdf/CREC-2015-06-08-pt1-PgS3866.pdf (accessed August 6, 2017).

Congressional Record Volume 161 (June 10, 2015), page H4040, et seq. https://www.gpo.gov/fdsys/pkg/CREC-2015-06-10/pdf/CREC-2015-06-10-pt1-PgH4040.pdf (accessed August 6, 2017).

Congressional Record Volume 161 (July 22, 2015), page S5473, et seq. https://www.gpo.gov/fdsys/pkg/CREC-2015-07-22/pdf/CREC-2015-07-22-pt1-PgS5473-2.pdf (accessed August 6, 2017).

Congressional Record Volume 161 (August 4, 2015), page S6300, et seq. https://www.gpo.gov/fdsys/pkg/CREC-2015-08-04/pdf/CREC-2015-08-04-pt1-PgS6300.pdf (accessed August 6, 2017).

Congressional Record Volume 161 (September 9, 2015), page S6478, et seq. https://www.gpo.gov/fdsys/pkg/CREC-2015-09-09/pdf/CREC-2015-09-09-pt1-PgS6478-2.pdf (accessed August 6, 2017).

Congressional Record Volume 161 (September 29, 2015), page. H6337, et seq. https://www.gpo.gov/fdsys/pkg/CREC-2015-09-29/pdf/CREC-2015-09-29-pt1-PgH6337.pdf (accessed August 6, 2017).

Congressional Record Volume 161 (November 4, 2015), page H7686, et seq. https://www.gpo.gov/fdsys/pkg/CREC-2015-11-04/pdf/CREC-2015-11-04-pt1-PgH7686.pdf (accessed August 6, 2017).

Congressional Record Volume 161 (November 5, 2015), page H7747, et seq. https://www.gpo.gov/fdsys/pkg/CREC-2015-11-05/pdf/CREC-2015-11-05-pt1-PgH7747-5.pdf (accessed August 6, 2017).

Congressional Record Volume 161 (November 16, 2015), page H8171, et seq. https://www.gpo.gov/fdsys/pkg/CREC-2015-11-16/pdf/CREC-2015-11-16-pt1-PgH8171.pdf (accessed August 6, 2017).

Congressional Record Volume 161 (December 1, 2015), page H8679, et seq. https://www.gpo.gov/fdsys/pkg/CREC-2015-12-01/pdf/CREC-2015-12-01-pt1-PgH8679-2.pdf (accessed August 6, 2017).

Congressional Record Volume 161 (December 2, 2015), page H8894, et seq. https://www.gpo.gov/fdsys/pkg/CREC-2015-12-02/pdf/CREC-2015-12-02-pt1-PgH8894-2.pdf (accessed August 6, 2017).

Congressional Record Volume 162 (May 25, 2016), page H3117, et seq. https://www.gpo.gov/fdsys/pkg/CREC-2016-05-25/pdf/CREC-2016-05-25-pt1-PgH3117-2.pdf (accessed August 6, 2017).

Congressional Record Volume 162 (June 7, 2016), page S3547, et seq. https://www.gpo.gov/fdsys/pkg/CREC-2016-06-07/pdf/CREC-2016-06-07-pt1-PgS3547.pdf (accessed August 6, 2017).

Congressional Record Volume 163 (July 12, 2017), page H5534, et seq. https://www.gpo.gov/fdsys/pkg/CREC-2017-07-12/pdf/CREC-2017-07-12-pt1-PgH5534-3.pdf (accessed August 6, 2017).

Info on IRS § 501(c)(3) Exempt Organizations:

Ardoin, Elizabeth. *Organizational Test-IRC 501(c)(3)*. U.S. Internal Revenue Service. http://www.irs.gov/pub/irs-tege/eotopicd04.pdf (accessed August 6, 2017).

U.S. Internal Revenue Service. *Tax Information for Charities & Other Non-Profits.*
https://www.irs.gov/charities-non-profits (accessed August 6, 2017).

U.S. Internal Revenue Service, *IRS Publication 4220. Applying for 501(c)(3) Tax-Exempt Status.*
http://www.irs.gov/pub/irs-pdf/p4220.pdf (accessed August 6, 2017).

U.S. Internal Revenue Service, *IRS Publication 3833. Disaster Relief: Providing Assistance Through Charitable Organizations.*
http://www.irs.gov/pub/irs-pdf/p3833.pdf (accessed August 6, 2017).

U.S. Internal Revenue Service, *IRS Publication 557. Tax-Exempt Status for Your Organization.*
http://www.irs.gov/pub/irs-pdf/p557.pdf (accessed August 6, 2017).

U.S. Internal Revenue Service, *IRS Publication 1771. Charitable Contributions: Substantiation and Disclosure Requirements.* http://www.irs.gov/pub/irs-pdf/p1771.pdf (accessed August 6, 2017).

U.S. Internal Revenue Service, *IRS Publication 3833. Disaster Relief: Providing Assistance Though Charitable Organizations.* http://www.irs.gov/pub/irs-pdf/p3833.pdf (accessed August 6, 2017).